UNDERSTANDING
MARSHA NORMAN

UNDERSTANDING CONTEMPORARY AMERICAN LITERATURE

Matthew J. Bruccoli, Founding Editor

Linda Wagner-Martin, Series Editor

Also of Interest

Understanding August Wilson, Mary L. Bogumil
Understanding David Mamet, Brenda Murphy
Understanding Lee Smith, Danielle N. Johnson
Understanding James Leo Herlihy, Robert Ward
Understanding John Guare, William W. Demastes
Understanding Neil Simon, Susan Koprince
Understanding Norman Mailer, Maggie McKinley
Understanding Sam Shepard, James A. Crank
Understanding Suzan-Lori Parks, Jennifer Larson
Understanding Tennessee Williams, Alice Griffin

UNDERSTANDING MARSHA NORMAN

Lisa Tyler

THE UNIVERSITY OF SOUTH CAROLINA PRESS

Published by the University of South Carolina Press
Columbia, South Carolina 29208

www.sc.edu/uscpress

Manufactured in the United States of America

28 27 26 25 24 23 22 21 20 19 10 9 8 7 6 5 4 3 2 1

Library of Congress Cataloging-in-Publication Data
can be found at http://catalog.loc.gov/.

This book was printed on recycled paper with 30 percent
postconsumer waste content.

ISBN: 978-1-64336-002-7 (hardcover)
ISBN: 978-1-64336-003-4 (ebook)

To Jim Tyler, with love

CONTENTS

SERIES EDITOR'S PREFACE

The Understanding Contemporary American Literature series was founded by the estimable Matthew J. Bruccoli (1931–2008), who envisioned these volumes as guides or companions for students as well as good nonacademic readers, a legacy that will continue as new volumes are developed to fill in gaps among the nearly one hundred series volumes published to date and to embrace a host of new writers only now making their marks on our literature.

As Professor Bruccoli explained in his preface to the volumes he edited, because much influential contemporary literature makes special demands, "the word *understanding* in the titles was chosen deliberately. Many willing readers lack an adequate understanding of how contemporary literature works; that is, of what the author is attempting to express and the means by which it is conveyed." Aimed at fostering this understanding of good literature and good writers, the criticism and analysis in the series provide instruction in how to read certain contemporary writers—explicating their material, language, structures, themes, and perspectives—and facilitate a more profitable experience of the works under discussion.

In the twenty-first century Professor Bruccoli's prescience gives us an avenue to publish expert critiques of significant contemporary American writing. The series continues to map the literary landscape and to provide both instruction and enjoyment. Future volumes will seek to introduce new voices alongside canonized favorites, to chronicle the changing literature of our times, and to remain, as Professor Bruccoli conceived, contemporary in the best sense of the word.

Linda Wagner-Martin, Series Editor

ACKNOWLEDGMENTS

I am grateful to Dr. Linda Wagner-Martin, series editor, for inviting me to propose a book for the *Understanding American Literature* series published by the University of South Carolina Press. I am also grateful to Dr. Linda Ginter Brown, who first sparked my interest in Marsha Norman more than twenty years ago when she asked me to consider writing about the Broadway musical adaptation of *The Secret Garden* for her pioneering essay collection on Norman's plays.

Sinclair Community College granted me a yearlong sabbatical that enabled me to work on the manuscript for this book. I deeply appreciate the luxury of having time to conduct research and write.

Finally, I would like to thank my family. My daughter, Rose, watched the episodes of *In Treatment* with me and read some of the chapters for me. My husband, Jim, reminded me of Marsha Norman as a promising subject for a book and patiently read every chapter before it was submitted. I hope they know how much I appreciate their love and support.

CHAPTER 1

Understanding Marsha Norman

Perhaps prompted by an interviewer's question (Beattie 292), American playwright Marsha Norman has described "trapped girls" as an important theme of her work, one that stems from her own childhood experiences growing up in a fundamentalist Christian family: "I saw myself as a trapped girl as a kid . . . trapped in this evangelical household full of violence" (Myers). Her mother, a fundamentalist Methodist, had a violent temper and strong religious beliefs. She forbade her children to watch television because of its perceived sinfulness, so Marsha spent much of her childhood reading. "I had a very isolated childhood, read a lot, played a lot and wasn't allowed to frown," Norman has said (Brustein 184). She often felt trapped in a hostile environment and later recalled longing to be kidnapped so that she could escape her family. Norman identifies the theme of the trapped girl not only in the character of Arlie in her first play, *Getting Out,* and Jessie in *'night, Mother,* but also in Mary Lennox in *The Secret Garden,* Celie Johnson in *The Color Purple,* and Francesca Johnson in *The Bridges of Madison County.*

Marsha Norman was born Marsha Williams in Louisville, Kentucky, on September 21, 1947, the first child of Bertha Connelly and Billie Lee Williams (Beattie 283). Her father was an insurance salesman who was rarely home because he regularly met with his clients in the evening (283). An extrovert, he enjoyed hunting and motocross racing. She had three siblings: Mark, who was three years younger; Stewart, six years younger; and Ruth, nine years younger. The family lived on Bourbon Avenue, between the Audubon Park neighborhood and the Louisville airport (283).

Her parents later joined a smaller fundamentalist group called the Christian Missionary Alliance. Norman, who found her mother's incessant praying off-putting, became skeptical at an early age. She once recalled that when she was eight, she heard a fire-and-brimstone preacher threatening the sinners in the congregation with the prospect of hell: "'Nothing this scary can be true,' she remembers thinking to herself" (Stout 30).

She felt that her mother never understood her and has said that her mother persistently bought dolls for her for Christmas, pretending that Marsha was the kind of daughter she really wanted (Craig 166). Her more sympathetic father, on the other hand, once gave her legal pads as a Christmas gift: "Best present I ever had," she said decades afterward (Brown, "Update" 189). Mrs. Williams would have preferred for her daughter to become a flight attendant and marry a doctor. She disapproved of her daughter's plays, which she saw as immoral. Norman has said, "She hated all my work—thought it was all vulgar, it was all filthy, it was all doomed—and my collective work was going to send me straight to hell" (Craig 170). Yet ironically, it was Norman's mother who first introduced Marsha to the theater by taking her to a production of *The Glass Menagerie* at the Actors Theatre of Louisville when Norman was twelve (Harriott 148). Norman has also credited her mother with giving her confidence that she could do whatever she wanted in life.

Norman felt closer to her great aunt, Bertha Toole, a working woman who never married. Part of what attracted her seems to have been the woman's glamour; Norman recalled that her great aunt "was always having her picture taken in bars and strapless red dresses" (Craig 166–67). Norman has called her "my patron saint and protector" (Beattie 283).

Norman dedicated her book *Four Plays* to Martha Ellison, her English teacher at Durrett High School, whom she later described (along with her great aunt and Olga Hanz, her piano teacher for many years) as one in a series of surrogate mothers who encouraged her to develop her talents. Ellison invited her to join the newspaper staff, encouraged her to enter contests, introduced her to the work of Lillian Hellman, and told her that she was going to be a writer (Beattie 287; Craig 167). Norman won a state writing competition her junior year, and her winning entry was published in the *Kentucky English Bulletin* (Stout 30). She had titled her essay "Why Do Good Men Suffer?" She later said that that theme was what she had written about her whole life (Beattie 387).

From 1965 to 1969, Norman majored in philosophy at Agnes Scott College in Decatur, Georgia, a small Presbyterian college for women (Beattie 287; Gussow, "Entering" 49). The liberal arts college had awarded her a music scholarship. She played piano for dance students each day and described her experience playing show tunes as "the beginning of my life in the musical theatre" (Beattie 288). Volunteer service in the children's burn unit at Grady Memorial Hospital in Atlanta as an undergraduate exposed her to the intense suffering of others early in life (Kane 257).

In 1969 she married Michael Norman, her former English teacher (Brown, *Marsha Norman: A Casebook* xv), and was hired to direct the children's unit at Kentucky Central State Hospital, a state mental hospital. She described herself as "completely unprepared" (Beattie 288). "Those two years of looking at people who had real trouble taught me more than I could have ever learned anywhere else about how people deal with trouble and what symptoms mean. I could see that the kid that was beating his head against the wall was not beating his head against the wall to make me unhappy or drive me crazy; he was doing it because that made it feel better. Somehow that act, which looked so bizarre, was actually simply that kid solving that problem that minute" (288). Her work there later inspired her first play, *Getting Out*.

Norman attended graduate school at the University of Louisville at night, eventually earning a master's degree in education in 1971. She later felt that apart from her music courses and a class on James Joyce's novel *Ulysses,* she had not really learned much during graduate school (290). From 1970 to 1972, she taught fifth grade at Prestonia Elementary School in the Jefferson County Public Schools' Advanced Program before moving on to be the "Filmmaker in the Schools" at J. Graham Brown School, where from 1972 to 1974 she taught children to make short eight-millimeter films as part of a special program of the Kentucky Arts Commission. She also completed what she has described as two thirds of another master's degree at the Center for Understanding Media, located in New York City (Stout 30).

In 1974 she and Norman divorced, although she retained his last name. As arts administrator for the Kentucky Arts Commission, she wrote a grant proposal for the Special Arts Project, secured the funding, and directed the program for two years. During her final year of the project, she also wrote for a Sunday children's supplement of the *Louisville Times* (Gussow, "Entering" 49; Steadman 692), and created a workbook for a Kentucky Educational Television program on basic reading skills. She earned enough money to take off work for a year to try and write.

Her first project was *Edison,* a musical about the American inventor Thomas Alva Edison, written for children. She sent it to Jon Jory, then producing director for the Actors Theatre of Louisville. He met with her and suggested that she interview Louisville residents about busing schoolchildren to integrate schools racially—then a highly controversial issue—in order to create a play from the raw material. She refused that offer, and he asked her what she wanted to write about instead. Norman's first play, *Getting Out,* evolved from her conversations with Jory.

The play, about a young woman's release from prison, was a triumphant success, especially for a first effort by a rookie playwright. Norman became playwright-in-residence at the Actors Theatre for the 1978–79 season and married Dann C. Byck, Jr., a theatrical producer and one of the theater's founders and first president, in 1978 (Steadman 691). Her second play, *Third and Oak,* premiered successfully at Actors Theatre in 1978; she wrote the screenplay when the first act, *The Laundromat,* was made into an hour-long HBO film starring Carol Burnett and Amy Madigan and directed by Robert Altman. The second act, *The Pool Hall,* was made into a 1989 television movie starring James Earl Jones and Mario Van Peebles.

Norman's third play, *Circus Valentine,* premiered at Actors Theatre in 1979 but was not a success. Inspired by the stories her grandfather told her when she was growing up, she wrote a comedy, *The Holdup,* which was given a workshop production in 1980 and then produced in San Francisco in 1983. Although it was not ultimately successful, she credits that play with teaching her techniques that helped her write her next play.

'night, Mother, her fifth play, won Norman the Pulitzer Prize for Drama in 1983. In the tense ninety-minute drama, uninterrupted by an intermission, a mother tries desperately to convince her adult daughter not to kill herself. The play premiered in Louisville and then moved to Broadway on March 31, 1983, at the Golden Theatre and played 380 performances. Kathy Bates and Anne Pitoniak starred in both productions; it made Kathy Bates a star. Norman also wrote the screenplay for the 1985 film of *'night, Mother* starring Sissy Spacek and Anne Bancroft. Although the play is now more than thirty-five years old, *'night, Mother,* which was revived in 2004, is still brought up in virtually every interview with Norman and will doubtless figure in her obituary someday.

In 1983 an excerpt from Norman's new musical, *Winter Shakers,* premiered at the opening night of the new Kentucky Center for the Arts (Gussow, "Critic's Notebook"). Set in 1857, the musical told the story of a man who convinces his wife that they should temporarily join the Pleasant Hill, Kentucky, Shaker community to get through the winter, only to lose her permanently to the celibate Shaker community (Mootz, "Marsha"). She and composer Norman L. Berman spent two years on the project. The *New York Times* reported that the musical was to be produced by the Off Broadway Circle Repertory Company (Lawson), but according to Norman, the production fell through when there was a change in management at the theater. "And eventually I lost interest in the piece as well," Norman has said. "I think contemporary audiences would have trouble believing that lots of folks would sign up to be members of a celibate community" (DiGaetani 250).

Norman's 1984 play *Traveler in the Dark* was so harshly reviewed that she has said that she did not write plays for four years afterward (*Marsha Norman: Collected Works* [abbreviated *CW* hereafter] 222). Instead she turned to another literary genre and wrote a novel, *The Fortune Teller,* which was published in 1987. Set within a twenty-four-hour period, *The Fortune Teller* is about Fay, the clairvoyant title character who believes she can help the police find a group of kidnapped schoolchildren. She also foresees her nineteen-year-old daughter, Lizzie, with a young man who wants to take her away forever. Each chapter tells the story of an hour in the search for the children.

Throughout her career, Norman has mentioned a series of unfinished or unproduced projects, including *Temptation,* a musical based on the life of twentieth-century evangelist and faith healer Aimee Semple McPherson (Mootz, "Marsha Norman Bounces Back"); *The Children with Emerald Eyes,* a 1979 screenplay for Columbia: a screenplay based on Gay Talese's bestselling novel *Thy Neighbor's Wife* for United Artists (Steadman 694); a musical based on the novel *Wuthering Heights* (Southgate); and a screenplay based on the now somewhat controversial 1981 novel *Medicine Woman* by Lynn V. Andrews (Harriott 159).

Norman and Dann Byck divorced in 1986 (Brown, *Marsha Norman: A Casebook* xvi). In 1987 she married Timothy Dykman, an artist, and the couple had two children, Angus and Katherine. She dedicated the book of the musical *The Secret Garden* first to her two children. Based on Frances Hodgson Burnett's 1911 novel that later became a childhood classic for many girls, Norman's musical *The Secret Garden* premiered at the St. James Theatre on Broadway April 25, 1991, and played for 709 performances. The production was nominated for seven Tony Awards and won three, including a Tony Award for Norman for best book of a musical.

Perhaps her most severe professional disappointment was *The Red Shoes,* a musical based on the 1948 British film of the same name about a ballerina torn between love and work. The musical closed on Broadway on December 19, 1993, after only five performances. It lost its producers nearly $8 million. In the aftermath of that humiliating public failure, Norman became seriously ill and was misdiagnosed with lung cancer—a terrifying experience that inspired her play *Trudy Blue,* written for the 1995 Humana Festival in Louisville. In part as a result of the reevaluation of her life caused by her brush with death, Norman and Tim Dykman were divorced in 1997. They both moved to Amagansett, New York, a small town east of East Hampton on Long Island, and shared custody of their two children (Southgate).

While her disastrous experience with *The Red Shoes* might have permanently discouraged a weaker playwright, Norman persevered in musical theater, moving on eventually to write the book for the musical *The Color Purple,* based on Alice Walker's 1982 novel, which won the Pulitzer Prize for fiction in 1983, the same year Norman won the Pulitzer for drama for *'night, Mother.*

The Color Purple: The Musical opened on Broadway on December 1, 2005 (after a series of previews in November), and played 910 performances at the Broadway Theatre, closing on February 24, 2008. It grossed nearly $104 million, according to Playbill Vault, and the production was nominated for eleven Tony Awards. Norman was nominated for a 2006 Tony Award for best book of a musical.

After the turn of the century, Norman became increasingly involved with writing for television. She wrote the screenplay for *Custody of the Heart,* a 2000 made-for-television movie starring Lorraine Bracco as a working woman whose stay-at-home ex-husband sues her for custody of their children. Norman also wrote the screenplay for *The Audrey Hepburn Story,* a made-for-television film starring Jennifer Love Hewitt as the title character. Norman wrote scripts for two 2007 episodes of the hour-long drama *Law & Order: Criminal Intent* and the teleplays for seven episodes focused on the character of Gina, played by Dianne Wiest, in the thirty-five-episode second season of the HBO television series *In Treatment,* which won a 2009 Peabody Award.

Yet despite her success in writing for television, Norman continued to return to her first love, the theater. Norman adapted Louise Erdrich's 2003 novel *The Master Butchers Singing Club* as a musical for the Guthrie Theater in Minneapolis, Minnesota. The novel is about German American immigrants in post–World War I North Dakota. The musical opened the Guthrie's 2010–11 season. Poor ticket sales forced the show to close a week early.

Norman also adapted *The Bridges of Madison County,* Robert James Waller's 1992 best seller, into a musical. *Bridges* opened at the Gerald Schoenfeld Theatre on Broadway on February 20, 2014, and played for one hundred performances. Norman was nominated for a Drama Desk Award in 2014 for outstanding book of a musical. The show began a national tour in fall 2015.

Norman is now eagerly sought out for the prestige of her presence. She has received honorary degrees from eighteen colleges and universities and served on the Board of Trustees of her alma mater, Agnes Scott College, from 2001 to 2011 (college website). She was honored with the William Inge Distinguished Lifetime Achievement in Theatre Award in 2011. Also in 2011, the United Nations commissioned Norman to write a play on human trafficking for its Theatre for Humans, an arts and entertainment production company devoted to educating the public about global problems through the performing arts (Myers). The play was given a reading at Juilliard on November 7, 2013 *(Theatre for Humans).*

As Norman herself puts it, "Even on the days when it has been most depressing, either a bad review or a lack of response or trouble with something I was trying to write or trouble with the other people around or whatever, writing is still the only thing I want to do at ten o'clock in the morning. . . . I am so fortunate in that the thing I most wanted to do in my life is the thing that I, in fact, do" (Beattie 296).

Influence and Legacy

Lillian Hellman is frequently cited as an important influence on Norman's work (Craig 173), although Norman herself has said, "I knew of no American women who wrote plays except for Jean Kerr and Lillian Hellman, neither of whom I wanted to become" (Norman, Introduction 2). Yet Norman began reading Hellman's work in high school and met Hellman in the summer of 1983, a year before she died (Burke 104), when Norman interviewed Hellman for "Articles of Faith: A Conversation with Lillian Hellman," an article that appeared in *American Theatre.* In that piece, she acknowledged, "Quite simply, I owe her a great debt" (Norman, "Articles" 364). Norman also praised Hellman in a 1984 article for the *New York Times* ("Lillian Hellman's Gift"). Sally Burke has since written at length about the relationship between the two writers, noting their shared southern heritage, "deep-seated connection to the South," interest in family drama, the theme of incest in their work, and the surrogate mothers who frequently appear in their plays, among other shared interests (106).

It is perhaps not surprising that, as a former philosophy major, Norman was strongly influenced in her craft by the Greek philosopher Aristotle: "Aristotle is very important to me. A while back, I learned that the rules really *are* the rules, and now I am not interested in breaking them or seeing how they could be stretched or changed" (Brustein190). Drawing on Aristotle's *Poetics,* European Renaissance classicists prescribed that playwrights should follow the three unities in crafting a play. Unity of time dictated that the action of the play should all take place within one day, and unity of place meant that a play should have a single setting. Unity of action meant that a play should have no subplots that did not contribute to the plot. Norman adhered faithfully to these unities in her early work, most notably in *Getting Out, Third and Oak,* and *'night, Mother.* She has also said that she believes that in tragedy, the protagonist must play a role in his or her tragic fate, a belief that echoes Aristotle's concept of *hamartia,* traditionally translated as the protagonist's "tragic flaw."

Norman has also cited other philosophers whose work has been important to her, including Kierkegaard and Plato (189). Among her other influences, Norman has named classic tragedies like Sophocles' *Oedipus Rex,* Euripides's *Medea,* Sophocles's *Antigone,* and William Shakespeare's *King Lear* (Brustein 190; DiGaetani 246), as well as classic plays such as Thornton Wilder's *Our Town* and Oscar Wilde's *The Importance of Being Earnest.* She also reads contemporary playwrights' work and cites Peter Shaffer, Sam Shepard, Simon Gray, Brian Friel (especially *The Faith Healer*), Christopher Hampton, and Lanford Wilson as playwrights whose work she admires (Brustein 190–91; DiGaetani 245–46).

Her name is frequently paired with that of Beth Henley (Gussow, "Entering"; Craig), also a southern-born playwright who had early work produced by the Actors Theatre of Louisville and who won the Pulitzer Prize. Both Norman and Henley are often linked with Wendy Wasserstein, "three talented playwrights of the same postwar generation" (Gussow, "Entering" 45).

Increasingly throughout her career, Norman has worked hard on behalf of the craft of playwriting. She has served as a vice president of the Dramatists Guild of America, a six-thousand-member association of professional playwrights, composers, lyricists, and librettists, and remains on its board of directors. For the first ten years of that organization's lifetime achievement award, she wrote the citations for the winners. She has also taught playwriting at New York University.

Norman and Christopher Durang together directed the Lila Acheson Wallace American Playwrights program at the Juilliard School in New York City for more than twenty years. Norman has mentored two Juilliard graduates who have become Pulitzer Prize–winning playwrights: David Lindsay-Abaire, who won for *Rabbit Hole* in 2007, and David Auburn, who won for *Proof* in 2001 (Thompson 14). Lindsay-Abaire joined Norman as codirector of the program when Durang stepped down in 2016 ("David Lindsay-Abaire").

She has written impassioned pleas for theaters to produce more plays by women playwrights, arguing, "We need to hear *all* the American stories, not half of them" (Norman, "Not There Yet" 79). She has found it disheartening that so many of her women students have found it tougher to get their plays produced than her men students have. "There may be a distinctly different gender view of what's a story and what's worth telling," she has suggested, noting that "Mel Gussow once said to me, 'Marsha, just look at your own plays. The ones that the critics like are the ones where the girls have guns'" (Garrison 40).

Norman and sister dramatists Julia Jordan and Theresa Rebeck founded the Lilly Awards, a nonprofit organization that celebrates women's accomplishments in American theater *(Lilly Awards)*. Named after American playwright Lillian Hellman, the Lilly Awards recognize excellence in producing, directing, composing, songwriting, and acting, as well as playwriting. The organization, under Norman's leadership as president, has launched an initiative to make summer writing colonies more family friendly so that women with children can participate. It has also funded a three-year study, in conjunction with the Dramatists Guild of America, called the Count, drawing on data from regional theaters throughout the United States to determine what kinds of plays are produced; the results indicated that only 22 percent of the plays produced were written by women, and a full account of the study and its results was published in the November/ December 2015 issue of the *Dramatist*, the official journal of the Dramatists Guild of America (*Lilly Awards*).

Themes

Norman writes dialogue in the language of ordinary speech, and even her darkest plays have moments of rich humor. Her plays (as distinct from her musicals) generally have small casts (Forman and Spencer 2491), and her characters are ordinary people—often the kind of women others overlook. "What I do are appearing acts, as opposed to vanishing acts. I really want to make visible people that are rarely seen and never heard," Norman explained (Stout 29). Elsewhere, she has described her work slightly differently: "In an odd way, writing for the theater is like nominating people for the archives of human history. As playwright, I select a person to nominate for permanent memory by the race" (Betsko and Koenig 329). Yet despite the ordinariness of the characters she depicts, she recognizes their extraordinary qualities: "I tend to write only about acts of courage" (Hatcher 188). She has talked about her plays as focused on the most important two hours in an individual's life: "They are about people who get to a certain point, where it is either go on or die, and the people ultimately find a way to go on. That moment, to me, is very thrilling. That is the reason to write, to pass along that kind of survival information" (Beattie 293). Not surprisingly, then, her plays are ultimately life-affirming: "Though the outcome may be tragic, the central character is usually personally triumphant" (Forman and Spencer 2491).

She has suggested that "the people in the plays are all the folks Mother wouldn't let me play with as a kid" (Harriott 158). What attracts her to the characters she chooses is their fundamental honesty: "For Norman's characters, the most important first lesson is to see things as they are" (132). Her characters are "people who need ultimately and finally to find out what the truth is, and who are willing to know it, whatever it costs them. They are not interested in suffering, they are not interested in pretending, and they want to know how things are. They want the real story" (152–53).

While she has repeatedly denied belief in God, Norman frequently writes about faith—most notably in *Traveler in the Dark* and *Sarah and Abraham*. Because of her mother's fundamentalism, Norman grew up learning Bible stories: "Those stories about the struggle between good and evil and why do good people suffer—those questions that the Bible asks over and over again—are questions that are still relevant to me" (Myers).

Many of Norman's plays concern parent-child conflicts—most obviously in *'night, Mother,* but also in *Getting Out, Traveler in the Dark,* her teleplay "Brother's Keeper" for *Law & Order: Criminal Intent,* and her screenplay for the television movie *The Audrey Hepburn Story.* She is particularly interested in the mother-daughter relationship, noting, "The things we as women know best have not been perceived to be of critical value to society. The mother-daughter relationship is a perfect example of that. It is one of the world's great mysteries; it has confused and confounded men and women for centuries and centuries, and yet it has *not* been perceived to have critical impact on either the life of the family or the survival of the family" (Betsko and Koenig 338).

In *Getting Out* and *The Color Purple,* she has examined the ways in which sexual abuse by a father figure has scarred her protagonists. But in many of her plays Norman is preoccupied with the lasting scars caused by family: "You can't escape where you were born, who you were born to and what you've inherited. This is a southern version of fate" (Savran 183). Norman has also broadened that sense of inevitability in her work, however, to encompass a sense of the living presence of the past, particularly evident in *Getting Out, The Secret Garden,* and *Loving Daniel Boone,* where onstage characters embody past selves, the dead, and the historical past, respectively. She is interested in dramatizing the ways in which people interact with their own past, be it personal, familial, or cultural.

Norman has suggested in one interview that "plays written by Americans are generally a child's view of what happens in that child's house. Unfortunately, most American dramatists don't write long enough to begin to write about anything else—say, to get fully into an adult's view of adultery" (Savran 190). Sam Shepard's *Fool for Love* is one exception she has named: "It will be wonderful if enough of us survive into writing about adultery. It's clear from looking at the English, who manage to keep their playwrights alive and working, that this is what happens next. Everybody writes about their marriages" (Savran 190). Certainly infidelity and the impermanence of romantic relationships constitute a theme that has long interested Norman, from *Third and Oak* through *Sarah and Abraham, Trudy Blue,* and *140* to *The Bridges of Madison County.* Since the births of her two children, she has also written about the conflicts women experience between work and family, most notably in *The Red Shoes, Trudy Blue,* and the teleplays *The Audrey Hepburn Story* and *Custody of the Heart.*

Throughout her career, Norman has evinced a strong interest in the emotional lives of women: "Like many recent women writers, Norman is more concerned with the interaction between women than with the intercourse between the sexes" (Rubik 141). She is particularly interested in women's friendships that cross class boundaries, as, for example, in her teleplays for *Face of a Stranger, Samantha: An American Girl Story,* and *A Cooler Climate.* Although she has sometimes resisted the label, she has consistently demonstrated a strong feminism in her work. As she herself somewhat irritably puts it, "If it's feminist to care about women's lives, yes, I'm a feminist writer" (Harriott 156).

It will be interesting to see what Norman, who is now in her seventies, will write next. As she herself has said, "Americans are increasingly having to deal with the ends of their lives. The end is lasting longer than it did. It's people like me who need to write about that" (Savran 191).

CHAPTER 2

"All the Help She Can Stand"

The Transformative Power of Women's Friendship in *Getting Out*

Getting Out deals with a young woman's painful, torturous passage through a series of liminal spaces: between prison and civilian life, between traumatic family life and the tenuous prospect of independence, and between a rebellious childhood self and a stoic and submissive adult self, both of which embodied selves are shown onstage simultaneously. In her introduction to *Getting Out*, Norman has credited Jon Jory, the producing director of Actors Theatre of Louisville, with the inspiration behind the work: "'Go back ten years in your life,' he said, 'to a time when you were physically frightened.' I knew instantly that I would write about a violent girl I had known briefly when I worked in a state mental hospital, a girl who later went to prison for murder" (*CW* 2). Their interactions were severely limited: "I only had an hour's worth of conversation with her in the entire time that I knew her. And that was mainly saying 'Don't destroy the furniture' to her, and her saying 'Fuck you!' to me," Norman said. "That was the entire content of our relationship" (Betsko and Koenig 337). She later told theater critic Mel Gussow, "This was a kid who was so violent and vicious that people would get bruises when she walked into a room" ("Women Playwrights").

Getting Out chronicles the immediate aftermath of the release of its twenty-something protagonist, Arlene Holsclaw, after serving an eight-year prison sentence at Pine Ridge Correctional Institute for Women. Arlene interacts with four visitors—her former guard, her mother, her former pimp, and her new neighbor—while the audience also sees her younger and much more volatile alter ego and past self, Arlie, experience an abusive childhood and an equally abusive incarceration. Inspired by Norman's experiences working in a state mental hospital in Kentucky, the play matter-of-factly dramatizes the extraordinary difficulties inherent in "getting out"—of prison, of sexually abusive and damaging family dynamics, of an exploitative heterosexual relationship, of a dangerous tendency to repeat familiar patterns, and of a self-denying religious belief system.

Norman has recalled sitting at the bar, unable to watch the premier performance, and feeling encouraged by the friendly comments she received at intermission: "But then at the end of the play, there was suddenly this incredible roar from the theater above us and I thought what the hell is that? And then the roar came down the back stairs. It literally felt like a train was coming toward me. The door opened at the other end of the bar, and this roar came into the room, which was actually all of these people who loved this play, and my old life and everything I had ever known was blown away by this roar" ("Marsha Norman and Donald Margulies" 25–26).

Theatre critic William Mootz has written, "Ask me what I remember as the most electrifying of all theatrical events that crowd my memory, and I have a ready answer. It was Actors Theatre's premiere of Marsha Norman's *Getting Out* on a chilly fall night in 1977" (qtd. in Ullom 55).

Despite the opening night audience's enthusiastic approval, however, more than one feminist scholar has criticized the play's ending as facile or inappropriately sunny. For example, in an article titled "The Impossibility of Getting Out," Gretchen Cline writes scathingly of the play's conclusion: "We are asked in this scene to forget the richness and complexity dramatized throughout and be assure that Arlene is now 'integrated.' . . . We are asked to trade in an experience of Arlene as painfully complex for the smile of an individual against all odds" (24). Theatre scholar Jenny S. Spencer has made a similar point: "Arlene may get out of prison, but her tragic plight involves a socially constructed identity that assigns her permanently to a powerless, passive position, to a female 'self' she hardly recognizes. . . . Represented here in extreme and inescapable form, the issues of sexual identity directly address the female audience member and make the experience of the play for her a thoroughly depressing one" ("Marsha Norman's She-Tragedies" 156).

Spencer professes amazement at "critical comments that assume we 'root' for Arlene or find any comfort in the notion of her 'making it'" (165n17). Spencer offers a much bleaker assessment: "The end of the play suggests that Arlene, at best, will survive the damage done to her" (156). But as Spencer herself concedes, the reviews of the play make it clear that audiences *did* "root" for Arlene to make it. Spencer contends that to do so, audiences "might see

Arlene's struggle precisely as the Board of Parole does—as a bad woman who is now good and whose prospects for 'reintegration' are promising" (165). In other words, Spencer contends that only by acting in bad faith can an audience root for Arlene.

But that's not the only possibility audiences—or Norman, for that matter—might envision for Arlene. The audience sees exactly how the repeatedly abused and traumatized Arlie has become the disaffected Arlene. But the audience does not want Arlene's story to end there. Norman has said that her plays "are all about people of great courage. They are about people who get to a certain point, where it is either go on or die, and the people ultimately find a way to go on. That moment, to me, is very thrilling. That is the reason to write, to pass along that kind of survival information" (Beattie 293). Elsewhere, she has added, "I tend to only write about acts of courage. . . . I see somebody doing something that I think is a really powerful move, and I know that it's not generally recognized as a powerful move. I know that it's my task as a playwright to get it into the right category" (Hatcher 188).

Given that the stage directions indicate that *"The apartment must seem imprisoned"* (CW 5), and Arlene herself notices that the windows are barred, it is certainly not irrational to perceive serious difficulty in ever really "getting out" of the situation in which she is enmeshed. But it is also not irrational to think that perhaps Norman knew what she was doing and that her play's ending cannot solely be ascribed to her own "unconscious defenses" (Cline 23). Surely the audience need not accept the dismal predictions of Arlene's pimp as the only accurate assessment of Arlene's prospects.

Throughout her life, Arlene—or more accurately, Arlie—has had no autonomy. What her new neighbor Ruby offers her is the limited self-determination available to a disadvantaged woman living in a patriarchal society, and what the audience roots for is that Arlene will learn to take advantage of that opportunity. Norman depicts Arlene as refusing three temptations, parallel to the three temptations of Christ as described in Luke (4:1–13) and Matthew (4:1–11). In making those choices for herself, she depicts Arlene as exercising autonomy for the first time in her life.

With the assistance of the Kentucky Prisoners Support Council, Norman interviewed both former inmates and prisoners at an institution called Pee Wee Valley in preparation for writing the play (Harriott 159). She recalled hearing announcements over a loudspeaker while there, noting, "All institutional announcements are the same" (159). The play opens with a "droning" disembodied voice stating the obvious ("Kitchen workers to the kitchen"—a line that Norman particularly relished) over the prison loudspeaker and then announcing that the library is closed for the day, the picnic table is off-limits, an exercise class is cancelled, and a picnic is postponed (*CW* 4). Clearly there is no possibility of rehabilitation here. An individual is directed to go to the gate for a visitor, but the anonymous speaker confuses two prisoners with similar-sounding names: Frances Mills and Frankie Hill. Individual identity is no longer important in this environment, and one woman prisoner is more or less interchangeable with another.

Significantly, Arlie later asks about Frankie Hill, one of the two women named in the anonymous droning prison announcements, and the guard Bennie tells Arlie that Frankie is "gone." When Arlie asks, "Out?" Bennie responds, "Pretty soon," and when Arlie presses him for the exact date of Frankie's upcoming release, he responds jocularly, "Miss her, don't you? Ain't got nobody to bullshit with. Stories you gals tell . . . whoo-ee!" (45). Unlike the prison announcer whose disembodied voice opens the play, Arlie does not consider Frankie interchangeable with any other prisoner. Arlie recounts what Frankie said about what she wanted to do first after her release, the simple domestic activity of mowing the grass, and it is clear the two had become close friends. But Frankie has evidently changed, at least in Arlie's eyes: "They done somethin' to her. Took out her nerves or somethin'. She . . ." (46). Bennie says, "She just got better, that's all" (46), but it's clear that Arlie does not see her friend as having changed for the better. On the contrary, Arlie describes Frankie as more or less lobotomized, in a way reminiscent of the central character in *One Flew over the Cuckoo's Nest*.

Arlie is an unlikely Christ figure. The audience learns of Arlene's prison record before meeting her. She is clearly a hardened case; she served her time in Alabama for a murder committed during a gas station robbery and attempted kidnapping on her escape from an earlier three-year term in Lakewood State Prison for forgery and prostitution, and she evidently has a substantial juvenile record in Kentucky. Somehow more disturbing than the institutional records regarding her crimes, however, is the chilling story her younger counterpart, Arlie, tells us, a sadistic tale of murdering the neighbor boy's pet frogs by throwing them into the street to be run over by passing cars and then laughing at the boy's horror. So when Arlene soon afterward tells Bennie, "I ain't as mean as I was" (6), the audience is initially relieved.

Only gradually does the audience learn that Arlie was sexually abused by her father. She rewards herself with money from her mother's purse afterward—thus launching her prostitution career. As a child, Arlie alleged that her father forced her to watch her parents having sex on a family camping trip (22). Her father beat both Arlie and her mother and evidently also sexually abused her sister, June, as Arlene's mother reveals: "Least bein' locked up now, he'll keep off June till the baby gits here" (15). Not surprisingly, all four of her siblings show evidence of psychological damage, engaging in a range of illicit behavior: promiscuity, prostitution, drug sales, theft, and assault with a knife.

Through intricate patterning, Norman suggests that Arlene is more like her mother than she might want to recognize (Bigsby 217). Arlene's father brought her mother chili and jelly doughnuts just as the principal promises Arlie peanut butter and chili if she will stay in school. Immediately after Arlene's mother says "Arlie, I'm waitin'. *(For the water.),*" the audience hears Arlie, in another time, say, "'Sides, I'm waitin'" (*CW* 22). As Christopher Bigsby notes, "Her mother complains that Arlene is skinny and her hair a mess only for Arlene to defend her mother against precisely the same attack (while a moment later denouncing her 'ugly hair')" (217). He suggests that it is not coincidental that Mrs. Holsclaw once cut hair, Arlene's sister Candy stole wigs, and Arlene learned to cut hair while she was in prison "as if she wished to be in a position to rectify this flaw in her mother's, and her, appearance" (217). Even Arlie's and Arlene's positions in the final scene echo Mrs. Holsclaw's: "*. . . both standing as Mama did, one hand on her hip*" (*CW* 58).

Arlene's mother repeatedly rejects her during her visit, but the first rejection is overtly physical. The stage directions indicate, "*Arlene moves as if to hug her. Mother stands still, Arlene backs off*" (14). Mrs. Holsclaw sweeps out the apartment but will not let Arlene have the broom. Arlene makes what the stage directions indicate is "*A very serious request*": "Maybe I could come out on Sunday for . . . you still make that pot roast?" (20). Her mother changes the subject. Arlene later tries again, saying, "I'll probably git my Sundays off," and her mother responds, "Sunday . . . is my day to clean house now" (21). Arlene's "requests" are so oblique and indirect that, as an audience, we are not entirely sure whether her mother even recognizes them as requests until later she yells at her daughter, "You're hintin' at comin' to my house for pot roast just like nuthin' ever happened, an all the time you're hidin' a goddam guard under your bed" (25).

Whereas Christ's first temptation was to make bread out of stones to appease his own hunger after a fast, Arlene's is to expect her stony-hearted mother to make pot roast to relieve Arlene's hunger for affection after a long stint in prison. The pot roast Arlene requests is both literal—the all-American comfort food—and symbolic—a stand-in for the nurturing she unsuccessfully seeks from her indifferent mother. Eager to find fault, Arlene's mother has by that point criticized first her daughter's thinness and then her hair (14), homophobically accused her of lesbian activity during her time in prison (21), refused to invite her to visit because Arlene would be a "bad example" to her two siblings still at home (21), and upon finding Bennie's hat under the bed, leaped to the conclusion that Arlene is still turning tricks because, as she tells

Arlene, "No man alive gonna drive a girl five hundred miles for nuthin'" (24). She mocks her daughter's request to be called Arlene and rips a twenty-year-old bedspread off the bed because her grown daughter did not say "thank you." The stage directions indicate that—not surprisingly—Arlene is *"Beginning to know how this is going to turn out"* (25).

As Sally Burke has suggested of Arlene's mother, "to embrace her daughter she would have to open her eyes to the sexual violence her husband inflicted upon Arlie and see what was truly hiding in her own bed all those years ago" (109). It is particularly chilling that Norman has openly acknowledged that the mother in *Getting Out* is her own mother. Norman recalled with astonishment that her mother once broke a window to get into Norman's sister's house to clean it (Craig 170). "When the mother in *Getting Out* walks in the door with a basket of cleaning supplies," Norman said, "I was convinced that Mother would know that this was a picture of her, because all she ever did was clean. I mean, it's a religious activity, I think. Sort of trying to get the dirt out, getting rid of the sin and evil, that's masquerading as dirt on the floor. But you know, she wasn't able to do that" (Beattie 284–85).

Leslie Kane has explicated the symbolism of Mrs. Holsclaw's propensity to remove dirt: "Toting her cleaning agents, bug spray, and linens and scrubbing with great vigor, Mother metaphorically implies her desires to sanitize Arlene. But Arlie/Arlene is soiled beyond any whitewashing" (259).

Arlie's rage at her own victimization is intense and murderous. As a child, she ineptly tried to kill her father by putting toothpaste on his bologna sandwich (*CW* 19). Even as an adult, Arlene warns herself not to touch her mother: "'Cause you might slit Mama's throat" (26). It is not coincidental that the man Arlie killed was "a cabdriver like her father and mother" (Scharine 194). In the play's final anecdote, Arlie recalls being locked in the closet by her sister June when they were "playin' policeman" (*CW* 58). Unable to free herself from that early imprisonment, Arlie is locked there so long that she pees in all of her mother's shoes. Proud of her own resistance (and her relatively innocuous revenge upon a rejecting mother), both Arlie and Arlene laugh together in the play's final scene.

The family is only the first in a series of (patriarchal) institutions that fail Arlie: public education, Western medicine, the American justice system, Christianity (Cline 3). Unwilling to investigate why Arlie acts out, the school principal angrily dismisses her from a regular public school and sends her to a special institution, presumably one for juvenile delinquents, telling Arlie, "they're used to your type over there" (*CW* 18). The prison doctor dispatches her to three weeks in isolation when she responds violently after a male inmate taunts her and drops his pants in a crude sexual invitation (26). The justice system, too, sees Arlie as aggressor, never as victim. Its indifference to prisoners is evident when we learn that Arlene was trained to cut hair in an Alabama state prison even though ex-cons cannot get a beautician's license in the state of Alabama (Scharine 194; *CW* 18–19). Even Arlene's mother concedes that Arlie came out of each juvenile institution worse than when she went in (*CW* 22).

The men in this play refuse to see her as a fellow human, insisting again and again that she is an animal. "She needs a cage," Evans tells Bennie (37). Evans later asks Bennie, "You screwin' that wildcat?" (38). Similarly, Bennie later calls her, "Screechin' wildcat" (46). When Bennie calls her "wild," Arlene explicitly rejects the dehumanizing characterization, quoting the prison chaplain: "Animals is wild, not people. That's what he said" (8).

Initially, from what Arlie reveals, the prison chaplain sounds like an exception: unlike her father, the pimp Carl, the prison doctor, or the prison guards, the chaplain is a moral man who seems to treat her with respect and perhaps even kindness. He calls her Arlene rather than Arlie, gives her a Bible with her name on the front, and introduces her to the teachings of Christianity. Although one scholar repeatedly refers to him as a "priest" (Cline 11–12), there is no indication within the play that the chaplain is Roman Catholic. On the contrary, given the prison's location in Alabama, a Protestant minister seems much more likely; Alabama has a minuscule Catholic population. Nationwide, more than 70 percent of prison chaplains are Protestant, while only 13 percent are Catholic, according to the Pew Research Center ("Religion in Prisons"). The chaplain's emphasis on reading the Bible—rather than, say, confessing her sins or praying the rosary—also suggests he is from a Protestant denomination.

The prison chaplain encourages her to reject that part of herself that causes trouble: "This chaplain said I had . . . said Arlie was my hateful self and she was hurtin' me and God would find some way to take her away . . . and it was God's will so I could be the meek . . . the meek, them that's quiet and good an git whatever they want . . . I forgit that word . . . they git the earth" (*CW* 54, ellipses in original). It is Ruby who offers the word Arlene can't recall: "Inherit" (54). As Margarete Rubik points out, "She can hardly repeat his antiquated Biblical phrases, let alone understand them" (144).

She struggles to read the Bible he gives her. The light bulb is broken, so she can barely see the pages. She has difficulty with unfamiliar words like "dwell." Ironically, Arlie is stumped altogether by the word "forsaketh" as she reads Psalms 37:27–29: "Depart from evil, and do good; and dwell forevermore. For the Lord loveth judgment, and forsaketh not his saints; they are preserved forever: but the seed of the wicked shall be cut off. The righteous shall inherit the land, and dwell therein forever." Arlene recites a shortened version of the verse's second sentence successfully later in the play (52).

The chaplain is abruptly transferred, but he does not bother to communicate news of his departure to Arlie. Bennie suggests to Arlene that the chaplain was "pretty leery of you" (8), which might explain why he does not meet with her before he leaves: he might have been afraid of her reaction. When one of the guards, Caldwell, eventually tells Arlie that the chaplain was transferred, Arlene becomes even more incoherent than her younger counterpart—"He said the meek, meek, them that's quiet and good . . . the meek . . . As soon as Arlie . . ."—and Arlie experiences a self-destructive breakdown. She spends three nights "screamin' to God to come git Arlie and kill her" (CW 53). In the play's horrifying climax, the audience learns that Arlene, in a suicidal fit of self-hatred, stabbed herself repeatedly with a smuggled fork, trying to kill the part of herself she knew as Arlie: "Arlie is dead an it's God's will" (54). She was hospitalized in the prison infirmary and nearly died. Even the prison staff are oddly impressed by her violence against herself; Bennie tells her, "Listen, ever prison in Alabama's usin' plastic forks now on account of what you done" (8).

According to Matthew, Christ's second temptation was to jump from a great height and rely on angels to save him. Arlene's second temptation is not just to travel from Alabama to Kentucky with Bennie, her former prison guard, but to rely on him to take care of her financially. Bennie seems friendly, and the audience, like Arlene, might initially be taken in by his apparently disinterested helpfulness. So it is particularly shocking when he tries to rape Arlene. Bennie's ulterior motive makes it clear he has little interest in Arlene's autonomy.

On the contrary, Bennie encourages self-surveillance. The Johnny Cash song "I Walk the Line" is about a man who chooses to be very careful about his emotions and (presumably sexual) behavior out of loyalty to a woman he loves. Bennie sings a parodic version of the song in which he invites the listener to untie the twine holding up his trousers. In this context (sung by a former prison guard to a female parolee), it is hard not to hear the song—which Norman, tellingly, misidentifies as "I'll Toe the Line" (44)—as celebrating a form of feminine self-surveillance. It is Arlie, not Bennie, who must keep her eyes wide open all the time. The fact that Arlene's neighbor Ruby has a picture of Johnny Cash on her door suggests that she has absorbed this particular lesson well herself.

Christ's final temptation was to worship the devil in order to gain the kingdoms of the world, whereas Arlene's final (and most tempting) temptation is to rejoin Carl, the violent and exploitative pimp whose crimes put her in prison in the first place, in order to have the money to send gifts to her son. According to Arlene, Carl was responsible for the forgery charge that sent Arlie to prison for the first time, and he fathered Joey, the child she was forced to give up to foster care. The fact that she has not told Carl that Joey is his child suggests that she is well aware of Carl's failings. He is much like her father: her mother describes Arlie's father as "sloshed" (19), and Carl as a "junkie" (22). Just as Ray Holsclaw has not driven the family cab in the last six or seven years, leaving his wife to become the family's breadwinner, Carl expects Arlie to return to prostituting herself and (in Mrs. Holsclaw's words) "sellin' the stuff he steals" (22) to provide him with money to live on. After a first meeting with the parasitic Carl, Bennie shrewdly tells Arlene, "Those types, just like the suckers on my tomatoes back home. Take everything right outta you" (30). While Bennie is right about Carl's exploitative nature, however, Bennie is in the end more like Carl than he wants to admit. Both men point out to her bluntly that she does not know anyone who is nice, anyone who is not a convict.

During his initial appearance in the play, Carl kicks in Arlene's door, rummages through her purse, and knocks her chicken dinner off the counter. He says he will not wear her out; he'll just expect her to handle "Four tricks a night" (27). Stage directions characterize Carl as *"Threatening,"* mention his *"vicious, sadistic laughter"* at Arlene, and indicate, *"He knocks her away and onto the bed"* (47–48). He throws the sweaters she has knitted into the sink; he swipes cookies from her grocery bag and throws the rest of the package on the floor. When he first arrives, Arlene calls his name, and he responds, "You 'spectin' Leroy Brown?" (27). Carl evidently aspires to be "the baddest man in the whole damn town," in the words of the song's refrain (Croce).

No wonder Carl claims that Carlsbad Caverns are named after him. Clearly, Arlie is right to refuse to tell him he is Joey's father. Heartbreakingly, young Arlie cannot sing the lullaby "Rock-a-bye, Baby" to Joey because she does not know enough of the words—a vivid representation of how little nurturing Arlie herself has received throughout her childhood. Not surprisingly, she cannot envision a future in which her son would be safe.

When Carl mercilessly dissects Arlene's bleak economic prospects, noting with grim accuracy how little money she is likely to make as a dishwasher and how much more she could make prostituting herself, Arlene is understandably discouraged by the picture he paints of her future. It is at this point that she comes closest to wavering, especially when Ruby confirms what Carl has said. It is only with Ruby's arrival—and apparent contempt for the man after she witnesses his *"rough treatment"* of Arlene (51)—that Arlene is finally able to send Carl away. She sees through him much more easily now. She recognizes that he is addicted (presumably to cocaine, given his sniffing), predicts that he will soon steal a car or beat up a junkie, and warns him that he will inevitably be caught for breaking out of jail.

Similarly, after Bennie returns with sad-looking petunias as an apology for nearly raping Arlene earlier, Ruby is the one who firmly insists that he leave. And

Ruby is the one who hesitantly warns Arlene that her sister Candy's johns may come looking for *her.* Given Norman's fundamentalist Christian upbringing, Ruby's name seems significant, recalling Proverbs 31:10 in the Authorized (King James) Version of the Bible: "Who can find a virtuous woman? For her price is far above rubies." In the Book of Matthew, angels minister to Christ once they drive out the devil—a clear parallel to Ruby, who sends both the men away and then tends to Arlene during her emotional breakdown. If we accept that these parallels are not an accident, they suggest that Arlene is not just surviving her trials, but triumphant. If this reading seems overly biblical for a woman who rebelled against her parents' fundamentalist Christianity, it is important to note that Norman did not reject all forms of Christianity: "Inasmuch as you have done it and to the least of these, my brethren, you have done it unto me," Norman quotes from the Gospel of Matthew. "That's what I'm doing. I'm saying, 'Let's take the least of these, our brethren. Let's look at them.' That's simply very important to me" (Stout 32). It would be difficult to argue that the withdrawn Arlene—sexually abused by her father, exploited by her boyfriend/pimp, traumatized and imprisoned—is not among the "least of these."

Perhaps one of the most encouraging signs of Arlene's progress away from her spectacularly dysfunctional family and traumatizing past is her question for her mother: "What kind of meat makes a pot roast?" (*CW* 25). Interestingly, her mother answers that question without hesitation: "Buy a roast. Shoulder, chuck . . ." (25). Norman here implies that Arlene will try to cook a pot roast for herself. If the pot roast represents maternal nurturing, the implication is that Arlene has given up hoping to receive that from her indifferent mother and is at least contemplating the healthier idea of providing that nurturing for herself instead. As Norman has said with respect to her own family, whose values she offended with "profane" plays such as *Getting Out,* "There comes a moment when we have to release our parents from our expectations" (Gussow, "Women Playwrights").

Arlene's insistence on her full name suggests that she wants a fresh start, a new identity, one distinct from the old Arlie, who was both a victim and a victimizer. As she pointedly tells Bennie when he calls her "Arlie girl," "Arlie girl landed herself in prison. Arlene is out, okay?" (*CW* 7). She wants to be the person the chaplain saw in her, even if it means killing part of herself. She has kept the *"cheaply framed picture of Jesus"* that the chaplain left her, even when Bennie points out that the chaplain probably "got it for free" (10), and she asks Bennie to hang it in a prominent place where she will see it every morning when she wakes up. She even spot cleans it when she notices a bit of dirt (45). When Carl snatches the picture down, she takes it from him and returns it to its place on the wall (49).

Tellingly, when Mrs. Holsclaw sees the picture of Jesus, she asks Arlene, "That your picture?" (20). The question is deliberately ambiguous, potentially meaning both "Does that picture belong to you?" and "Is that a picture of you?." Arlene acknowledges, "The chaplain give it to me," and her mother, after realizing the picture is from the same chaplain who called her daughter Arlene rather than Arlie, says, "It's crooked. *(Doesn't straighten it.)*" (21). Mrs. Holsclaw knows her daughter is "crooked"—meaning both criminal and warped by her upbringing—and has no intention of trying to help her straighten herself out.

Norman suggests that the surest way out for Arlene is to acknowledge her circumstances with honesty and to learn from Ruby, a fellow ex-con who offers her kindness and advice without ulterior motives. Unlike the male characters, who insist on calling her "Arlie" despite her insistence that she is "Arlene" now, Ruby recognizes that "Arlie" is gone but gently tells Arlene that she can still mourn what she has lost. When Arlene becomes distraught, *"grieving for [her] lost self,"* it is Ruby who consoles her: *"Ruby continues to hold her tenderly, rocking as with a baby"* (55). Ruby tries to warn Arlie against future dangers by sharing a story of how a naïve waitress was duped by an unscrupulous and exploitative man, although Arlene sees through the ruse of "this waitress" and asks Ruby if she served time for her mistake. Near the end of the play, Arlene's reference to the card game "Old Maid" suggests that she prefers Ruby's supportive company to the violence and coercion of Carl's or Bennie's. The stage directions indicate that Ruby's reaction is ambivalent; it is *"Not her favorite game"* (57). Perhaps she would prefer a heterosexual relationship to old maidhood, but Ruby is lonely, too; even Old Maid is better than "beatin' myself all the time at solitaire" (44).

Janet Brown and Catherine Barnes Stevenson suggest that "much of the play's stage business involves [Arlene's] attempt to make a home" for herself and "the domestic becomes the nexus of [her] relationship to the other characters" (189). Tellingly, Ruby moves to pick up Arlene's groceries from the floor but stops herself, telling Arlene, "I 'magine you'll want to be putting these up yourself" (*CW* 52). Her careful recognition of Arlene's autonomy signals her difference from the oblivious Bennie, who responds to Arlene's repeated dismissals with "Thought I might help some" (56). As Ruby points out, "Arlene's had about all the help she can stand" (56). What she needs is not help but rather people who support her autonomy, even when it means letting Arlene perform the simplest actions on her own. When Arlene puts her groceries away *"Slowly, but with great determination"* at the end of the play (58), the audience knows that she has chosen autonomy. Despite its dark subject matter, the play ultimately celebrates the potentially transformative power of women's friendship in a patriarchal rape culture.

Getting Out "has been performed in prisons across the country" (Stout 32). The play was so successful that it was chosen for the Actors Theatre of Louisville's international tour (Ullom 67). It was then revived off Broadway in 1979 at the Theatre de Lys and ran for eight months.

"Years later, I would realize that I wasn't writing about Arlie, I was writing about myself," Norman states in the play's introduction. "I would realize that all of us are frequently mistaken for someone we used to be, but that's a story for another day" (*CW* 3). As she once told an interviewer, "The choices you make out of freedom are the best ones" (Betsko and Koenig 340).

CHAPTER 3

Early Plays

Third and Oak, Circus Valentine, and *Traveler in the Dark*

Third and Oak, a pair of one-act plays designed to be performed together, premiered at the Actors Theatre of Louisville in March 1978. Norman has written in her introduction to the two companion pieces, *The Laundromat* and *The Pool Hall,* in her *Collected Works:* "though each act is frequently performed by itself, I prefer that the two acts be seen together. Rather like the right foot following the left" (60). She has called the play "unproduceable" because "I got a bad piece of advice from someone who told me to split them apart into two plays, and the result was that they were seen as one-acts and not as a whole play" (Brown, "Update" 163). She justifies her preference for performing them together by alluding to what she sees as their shared theme: "These two plays are about the same thing: why we lie to protect ourselves when we could tell the truth and be saved. Not that the plays answer this question. Plays don't answer questions, they simply preserve them, they pass them on" (*CW* 60).

National Public Radio recorded both *The Laundromat* and *The Pool Hall* for its Earplay series of contemporary plays adapted for radio, and both are now readily available as MP3 files free online. *Third and Oak: The Laundromat* was part of the Ensemble Studio Theatre's One-Act Marathon in New York City the following December (59). In 1984 it was made into an hour-long HBO movie starring Amy Madigan and Carol Burnett (59). Five-time Oscar nominee Robert Altman directed. *The Pool Hall* was made into a television movie starring James Earl Jones and Mario Van Peebles by Nederlander Television

& Film. One of four hour-long plays by Pulitzer Prize–winning playwrights, it aired on the A&E cable television network in 1989 as a General Motors Mark of Excellence presentation called "American Playwrights Theatre" (Campbell). The other playwrights included in the series were Eugene O'Neill, Paul Zindel, and Tennessee Williams (Campbell).

Sorting Life's Problems, One Load at a Time

Third and Oak: The Laundromat

In a series of articles in *Esquire* magazine describing his personal battle with depression, American novelist F. Scott Fitzgerald wrote, "in a real dark night of the soul it is always three o'clock in the morning, day after day" (Fitzgerald 75). In Norman's play *Third and Oak: The Laundromat,* it is no accident that the action begins at 3:00 A.M.

Deceptively slight, this one-act play set in the late 1970s chronicles an encounter between two women, Alberta and Deedee, in an all-night laundromat located at the intersection of Third Street and Oak, where there once really was a twenty-four-hour laundromat in Louisville (Burke 105). Norman told one interviewer, "I used to see that laundromat on my way home in Louisville, after nights of parties at the theater. I would drive home, and there would be this laundromat in the middle of the night, [and] at two, three o'clock in the morning, there would be two people in there" (Beattie 294). She has also said that she wrote the play for Anne Pitoniak, the actress who played Arlene's mother in the premiere production of *Getting Out* and Thelma, Jessie's mother, in the premiere and Broadway productions of *'night, Mother.* Pitoniak played Alberta in the premiere production of *Third and Oak: The Laundromat.*

The play's laundromat setting is no accident. "As women, our historical role has been to clean up the mess," Norman has said. "We know that somebody has to clean it up, and that only if it is cleaned up can we hope to start over, and get better" (Betsko and Koenig 339). Moreover, as Esther Harriott notes, the "laundromat becomes a symbol for purging and redemption" (Harriott 138). Spencer goes on to note the significance of the women's activities: "the action is marked by the rhythm and tempo of domestic work. Thus conversations are motivated, maintained and framed by repetitive, unrewarding, interminable routines that in these plays constitute the sphere of female activity. Alberta and Deedee, for example, meet each other in one of the few places outside the home women might be found alone in the middle of the night" (Spencer, "Marsha Norman's She-Tragedies" 151).

In this play, Norman depicts women bonding over their own loneliness despite profound class and generational differences. Alberta, a retired schoolteacher in her late fifties, and Deedee, a "restless twenty-year-old" married to an autoworker (*CW* 60), would seem to have very little in common. Yet the fact that they share the same last name, Johnson, suggests that, as Deedee puts it, they "might be related" (*Third and Oak: The Laundromat* 9). Both women are unsteady: Alberta *"accidentally knocks over her purse,"* and Deedee *"trips over a wastebasket on the floor and falls over her laundry as it spills out of the shirt"* in which she has tied it (6).

Deedee's husband, Joe, is gradually revealed through her comments as a brutish lout whose behavior toward his wife verges on abuse. He refuses to laugh at her innocuous joke—"How often do you have to water a Ford plant?"—but would have laughed if she had tripped over the furniture (6). He once broke his toe kicking a chest of drawers in a fit of anger over a hole in his bowling shirt. "He thinks hangers are for when you lock your keys in the car," she tells Alberta (6). Although Deedee would like to start a family, he spends all their money on a '64 Chevy he wants to drag race. He quickly gives away the birthday present Deedee gives him, which tellingly is a doll with Deedee's face. When Deedee contemplates flirting with Shooter Stevens, the African American radio deejay whose broadcast words open the play, she takes a certain pleasure in flouting her husband's racism: "Joe hates black people," Deedee says, and he believes black people are all "thinkin' about killin'" (18). Ultimately, of course, Deedee reveals that she has discovered that her husband has been unfaithful to her.

Alberta repeatedly makes comments that foreshadow what she will eventually reveal about her husband, Herb: "He died last winter, the day before his birthday" (23). When Deedee suggests that Alberta should have her husband fix the washing machine she says is broken, Alberta poignantly responds, "It can't be fixed" (7). Of the laundromat's sleeping attendant, Deedee says, "You don't think he's dead or anything, do you? I mean, I probably wouldn't know it if I saw somebody dead," and Alberta laconically responds, "You'd know" (9). As she somewhat plaintively tells Deedee, "People can't always be where we want them to be, when we want them to be there" (16). When Deedee responds that she does not like it, Alberta counsels acceptance: "You don't have to like it. You just have to know it" (16). Her words gently remind the audience of the truism that all advice is autobiographical.

Perhaps the play's most moving moment occurs when Alberta tells Deedee, "I found our beachball when I cleaned out the basement. I can't let the air out of it. It's his breath in there" (24). Norman herself has said, "That play has the line everybody always says is the best one I've written." Norman elaborates: "To tell the truth, I didn't so much write the line as hear Annie [actress Anne Pitoniak] say it in my head and write it down" ("Anne Pitoniak"). The audience's reaction at the play's premiere reveals the line's haunting significance: "When the character spoke that line, recalls Mr. [Jon] Jory [of the Actors' Theatre], you could hear a sigh from the audience" (Gussow, "Women Playwrights").

What haunts both of these women is their own loneliness—the loneliness of the bereaved wife who misses her husband desperately and the loneliness of the betrayed wife whose husband treats her callously: "the opening theme song 'Stand By Your Man' underscores the pathetic and potentially absurd nature of the loyalty their behavior illustrates" (Spencer, "Marsha Norman's She-Tragedies" 160). Alberta suggests that Deedee should tell Joe how she feels, but Deedee is resistant: "He'd leave me" (*Third and Oak: The Laundromat* 21). "Maybe," Alberta responds, to Deedee's anger. Deedee can foresee the whole miserable conversation: "I don't want to start it. I don't want to say I want a real job, 'cause then I'll say the reason I want a real job is I gotta have something to think about besides when are you coming home and how long is it gonna be before you don't come home at all. And he'll say what do you mean don't come home at all and I'll have to tell him I know what you're doing. I know you're lying to me and going out on me and he'll say what are you gonna do about it. You want a divorce? And I don't want him to say that" (21).

Alberta begins one of the most telling exchanges in the play by insisting that she does not want Deedee to be alone, that that was not what she meant. Deedee responds, "Looks like I'm alone anyway," and Alberta says, "That's what I meant" (24). From Alberta's perspective, staying with the wrong man is worse than simply being alone. It is not an accident that the only one of Snow White's seven dwarves whose name Deedee cannot remember is Happy. She cannot even remember being happy.

Part of the reason Deedee puts up with the way Joe treats her is that she is used to it. Her own mother does not trust her to set the dryer heat properly and "borrows" from Deedee's money, which she leaves with her mother to protect it from Joe. Unlike Alberta, her mother is not sympathetic: "That's what mom always says, 'Cheer up'" (9). Deedee says that her mother never speaks to her when she visits; Deedee's mother thinks Joe is a bum and instead wanted her daughter to marry a man who had the potential to manage a drugstore someday. It is her mother who tells Deedee that the third year of a marriage is the "itch year" when men are likely to stray, even though it is traditionally the seventh year (Epstein 38). Deedee at first makes excuses for her mother: "she don't ever say how she likes seeing me, but she holds back, you know. I mean, there's stuff you don't have to say when it's family" (*Third and Oak: The Laundromat* 7). But eventually, when Alberta suggests that Deedee could go stay with her mother if she leaves Joe, it is no wonder that Deedee says, "She's the *last* person I'm tellin'" (22).

Deedee was not treated much better in high school, where she was bullied by boys as loutish as her husband: "Hey, Deedee, is Deedee your name or your bra size?" (11). One of the boys would ask another, "'Hey, did you have a good time last night?' And David would say, 'Yes. In Deedee.' Then they'd slap each other and laugh like idiots" (11). She has been victimized over and over by immature men.

Norman consistently uses dialogue to illuminate character: "Deedee is a nervous and compulsive talker. . . . While her unthinking chatter provides much of the play's humor, it also indicates the depth of her unhappiness and her inability to face it. Alberta, a former teacher, speaks precisely but reluctantly; and her conversation style quickly discloses the pattern of avoidance by which she suppresses her own emotional vulnerability" (Spencer, "Marsh Norman's She-Tragedies" 149).

Deedee eventually voices her own low opinion of Joe: "He's mean and stupid. I thought he'd get over it, but he didn't" (*Third and Oak: The Laundromat* 22). Alberta gently tells Deedee what anyone in an abusive relationship needs to hear: "You don't have to put up with what he's doing. You can if you want to, if you think you can't make it without him, but you don't have to" (23). She simultaneously recognizes Deedee's autonomy and encourages her to see that she deserves better treatment.

These women support each other empathetically through the most difficult crisis of each woman's life. Deedee tells Alberta, "I wish Mom were more like you," then adds, "Smart. Nice to talk to" (20). Alberta tells Deedee, "you're young and pretty. You have a wonderful sense of humor" (20) and later insists, "you are not dumb, child. And don't let anybody tell you you are, O.K.?" (23). After their initial prickliness, they are often carefully protective of each other's self-esteem.

Spencer suggests, "In a very real sense, nothing happens . . . the brief encounter between two women in *The Laundromat* provides a fleeting contact that changes neither woman's life" ("Marsha Norman's She-Tragedies" 148). But the audience cannot see the outcome of this encounter, cannot know whether their late-night exchange enables them to change their lives.

"Give Me a Break"
Third and Oak: The Pool Hall

In both the 1957 Broadway musical and 1962 film *The Music Man,* the con man Professor Harold Hill warns the people of River City, Iowa, that the presence of a pool table in their town is an irrefutable sign of trouble. Playing pool, he assures the townsfolk in the comic song "Trouble," will lead their sons to smoke, gamble, drink, and perhaps even fornicate. While this puritanical attitude is easy to satirize, it reflects a lingering prejudice about the dangers of the setting Norman chose for the second half of *Third and Oak:* a "small and seedy" pool hall.

The Pool Hall, which has been accurately described as "the lesser of the two plays" that make up *Third and Oak* (Stout 32), explores some of the same territory as Norman's other plays—including parent-child relationships, suicide, bereavement, and infidelity—from a male perspective. The play consists mostly of a dialogue between two African American men: Gary Wayne "Shooter" Stevens, a thirty-year-old radio deejay, and Willie, the owner of the pool hall, "who looks to be about 60" (*Third and Oak: The Pool Hall* 3). In an interview, Norman has said that she wrote the play for a specific actor: "Joe Morton was around the theater at the time and said, 'Why don't you write a play for me?' I would never have written *The Pool Hall,* never written a role for a young black man, had Joe Morton not invited me to do it" (Harriott 152). Norman attributed her ability to write dialogue for an African American man to her experience working as a teacher: "I spent some four years teaching film in an integrated alternative school that went from kindergarten to junior high, so there I was all day with black kids, from little kids to seniors, and you just pick up that language. And I do have that kind of ear—in seeing, they call it an eidetic memory or photographic memory. That's the kind of aural memory I have" (Harriott 152). She also conducted interviews to prepare to write the play (Betsko and Koenig 335).

In *The Pool Hall* a casual discussion between Shooter and Willie about handicapping horses leads by association to a more serious discussion of George, a "sick" older man to whom Shooter gave a leather-trimmed wheelchair (*Third and Oak: The Pool Hall* 6). Shooter gradually reveals that George is Sondra's father (and therefore Shooter's father-in-law). Willie gently acknowledges Shooter's generosity, and although Sondra has told Shooter that George would not even know that the trim on the wheelchair was real leather, Willie insists that George *does* know and appreciates Shooter's thoughtfulness.

George, Willie, and Shooter's father were always close friends—or, in Shooter's words, "More like triplets" (23). They once got into a melee at Willie's pool hall, and all three men landed in jail, where a cop gave them cheese to keep them quiet until Shooter's mother arrived to bail them out and gave them their nickname, the Three Blind Mice. Shooter's father, also known as Shooter because of his exceptional skill as a pool player, never held a real job, according to Willie, so George and Willie helped pay his bills. Shooter's father had a bad run at the pool hall one night and then jumped off a bridge to his death. Shooter asks Willie why his father jumped into a salvage yard rather than into the water, and Willie says, "He was a helluva swimmer," and "he didn't want to give himself the slightest chance of pullin' outta that dive alive" (13). His suicide has long troubled both his son and Willie (and very likely the unseen George, as well).

Perhaps in part because of his unresolved grief, Shooter experiences an early midlife crisis. He seems particularly discouraged by a caller to his radio show: "Little kid called me up tonight, wanted to talk to the record player. I said it don't talk, kid. He said, 'No, man, you man, the record player.' Over the air he said that" (7). He bitterly resents the idea that he is indistinguishable from the technology he uses. Willie belittles him further, telling him, "it don't matter what you say over the air" because "Folks turn on the radio to hear the music, remember?" (7). Shooter is worried about his professional future but cannot identify anything else he likes to do. Willie says, "There's about a billion jobs in this world. You think there ain't one or two might make you happy?" Shooter angrily replies, "You don't work to be happy. You work to make money. Happy, my man . . . was one of the seven dwarfs" (17). As in *Third and Oak: The Laundromat,* happiness is elusive.

Unlike the bowling alley bartender in *Third and Oak: The Laundromat,* who not only knows of Joe's infidelity but is complicit, assuring "Patsy" that "He's on his way" (21), Willie persistently urges Shooter to go home to his wife, Sondra, even though Shooter just as persistently resists Willie's suggestions. Willie is especially concerned because a man came in to the pool hall looking for Shooter, trying to collect on a six-thousand-dollar debt, which a disapproving Willie assumes must be for either illegal drugs or gambling. In spite of Willie, Shooter is flirting with exactly the kinds of trouble that the con man of *The Music Man* warned people against.

Shooter also flirts with Deedee—the young woman from *Third and Oak: The Laundromat*—when she walks into the pool hall. Not surprisingly, Willie abruptly and rudely attempts to end the flirtation. Shooter concedes that it is Willie's pool hall and offers to call her a cab (24), but after she leaves, he turns on Willie, asking what gives him the right to run Shooter's life. Furious, Shooter compares the older man to Moses—an archetypal law-giving patriarchal figure and angrily tells Willie that it will kill George if Willie closes the pool hall and retires to Asbury Park. Only then does Willie reveal that George is dying and has just six months left to live. Selling the pool hall, Shooter realizes, will give Willie the money to keep George comfortable during his final months.

Although Sondra calls to check on her father, she does not visit. Her reluctance stems from her fear of seeing him so ill and perhaps from her intuited recognition of the seriousness of his illness. As Willie says, "She's afraid she'll be with him when it happens" (29). Shooter offers an alternate explanation for Sondra's choices: "maybe she's just a selfish, silly girl who started buying grownup clothes but never grew into them" (29). Ironically, given his judgmental tone, Shooter did little better when it was his turn. When Shooter's father died, Shooter was in Miami Beach, so Willie had to identify the body, carry him to the ambulance, and pay for the funeral. Both Shooter and Sondra choose absence as their coping strategy. Neither of them is mature enough to handle a parent's death appropriately.

Perhaps Shooter's own immaturity explains why Sondra is unwilling to have a baby. As Willie points out to Shooter, "what you're doin' now, goin' out on her all over town, that's supposed to convince her to have your boy for you?" (20). Willie wants Shooter and Sondra to have a child for reasons that are at least partly selfish: "You don't have any children, it's the end of the line for the Three Blind Mice" (21). Shooter sees through Willie's smoke screen; when Willie says, "Shooter needs a grandbaby," Willie responds, "Shooter is dead. *(Now turning to face him.)* Willie needs the grandbaby" (21).

The play also includes an additional scene to be inserted into *Third and Oak: The Laundromat* when the two plays are produced together. In that scene, Shooter enters the laundromat and offers the women tacos. Deedee worries that the meat in the restaurant's tacos is dog food because she has seen dog food cans in the building's trash. Shooter smiles and suggests that maybe there's an actual dog. When Alberta suggests, "It could be someone else in the building," Shooter feels vindicated, but Deedee knows better: "She didn't mean they have a dog. She meant some old person in the building's eatin' dog food. It happens. A lot around here" (34). The exchange suggests the grinding poverty of the neighborhood in which both plays take place.

Shooter then offers Deedee a piece of fudge cake in an overt sexual overture that Deedee politely refuses. After his departure, the two women talk about Shooter's sudden appearance, which frightened both women momentarily because they thought he might be a criminal. Alberta seems particularly unnerved, although it is not entirely clear whether she simply disapproves of adultery or (as Deedee suspects) is particularly horrified at the prospect of an interracial sexual relationship—a prospect that also bothers Willie, who repeatedly asks Shooter about "white girls."

Throughout *The Pool Hall,* Willie struggles to parent Shooter, to encourage him to mature: "You gonna grow up if it kills you" (10). Shooter repeatedly tries to talk Willie into playing a game with him, and each time, Willie resists. At the end of the play, in its emotional climax, Willie unexpectedly offers to play pool with Shooter: "*Willie's offer is unexpected, it triggers an overwhelming emotional response in both of them. They embrace, acknowledging at last, their desperate need, their mutual loss, and their pure and lasting love for each other*" (29). As with *Third and Oak: The Laundromat,* the ending suggests that only through human connection can grief be resolved.

"A High-Risk Occupation"

Circus Valentine

Circus Valentine, an aesthetically unsatisfactory play that Norman later described as her "first failure" (*CW* 110), chronicles the decline of a financially strapped traveling circus when it abruptly loses its signature attraction, a juggling act performed by conjoined twins. Norman wrote *Circus Valentine* while she was playwright-in-residence for the Actors Theatre of Louisville, and it premiered at the Humana Festival of New Plays there in 1979 and ran for eleven performances (Stout 32; Steadman 693). It was not well received. As Norman herself somewhat hyperbolically wrote in her introduction to this play in her *Collected Works,* "This play has never been published before, or produced again since its premiere, a night of humiliation and failure so complete as to almost destroy my ability to remain in the theatre" (110).

She later came to value the experience, saying in a 1988 speech at Kenyon College, "*Circus Valentine* was how I learned to live this life" (*CW* 408). By then she was able to joke about it: "You can always tell which plays are not going to work, because your friends come up to you in previews and tell you the work is ambitious. Deadly, that word, ambitious. Ambitious means, Well, sweetheart, you tried" (399).

In the play Fred and Goldie Valentine, a married couple in their forties, run Circus Valentine. Norman's aptly titled play is genuinely a valentine to the traveling circus. Dramatic monologues from several of the characters—including Fred; Goldie; their former brother-in-law, Tony; their daughter, Trina; Goldie's sister, Eva, the aerialist; and finally Fred again—celebrate the glamour of the circus, the allure of the various acts, the challenges of behind-the-scenes life in a traveling circus, and finally circus people such as Fred's mother. Norman seems to have a special spot in her heart for the circus, which she has compared to theater, magic, and church services, all of which require a live audience to work: "You can't get this stuff on your Ipod. So these are things that stand a chance of surviving as live forms. . . . So these experiences that require us to actually be there to experience them, have a chance of continuing to be necessary. Some stories—you have to see them to believe them. That's what will keep us all working, I hope" (Garrison 42).

She has compared playwrights to trapeze artists: "The real people that belong in the theater know that, just *know* it. I'm sure that it's the same with great trapeze artists; there is probably some great thing that you have to know in your blood if you're gonna be a great trapeze star" (Hatcher 194).

When the performers express a certain anger at the uncomprehending audience, it is certainly possible that Norman shares that anger. Goldie says, "They don't care that we risk our lives for their money. They think we enjoy it. Karl Wallenda took his last walk for sixty lousy people" (*CW* 140). Norman has always taken risks as a playwright, and the consequences have been both good—a Pulitzer Prize, a Tony, financial success—and bad—harsh reviews, public humiliation, financial losses. It would not be surprising if she, like the circus performers, resented the audience's incessant demands for entertainment and complete ignorance of the difficulties the artist faces. As she said in her Kenyon talk, "You can be surprised by which plays they knock you off the wire for, but you have to be prepared. It is a high-risk occupation" (407).

Throughout the play Norman emphasizes the fictitiousness and artificiality of the circus. In Helen Stoddart's words, "The circus is mendacious" (1); it "benevolently deceives" (124). For example, in Norman's play, Goldie and Eva masquerade (not very successfully) as the missing conjoined twins. Eva "speaks in a fake Russian accent most of the time" (*CW* 110). Tony Navarro "is not Spanish" (110) but speaks *"in a mock Spanish accent"* (118). When Tony offers to do a springboard act to help flesh out the second act after the twins disappear, Fred introduces him as "Alberto Ajanian" (139). Goldie appears as "Mademoiselle Margobella," the juggler, but she is so inept that *"The balls all fall to the floor"* (145). Trina and Eva are introduced as "Ella and Elvira Esterhazy" (151). Identities are fluid and flexible in this world, and people can reinvent themselves over and over again—first performing a snake act, then masquerading as one of the conjoined twins, then flying as a trapeze artist. Names, professions, and overall identities are not as fixed as they often are in the non-circus world. Identifying it as "something essential about the circus," Stoddart has suggested that "an audience may always prefer either an enchanting or alarming fiction (well presented) over a bare-faced fact" (2).

The play has some funny moments, but it is overstuffed with enough plotlines for half a dozen plays. For example, Trina is attracted to Tony, who is twice her age, and she longs for a normal life, while Eva longs to attempt a notoriously dangerous triple somersault and anticipates with great sorrow the day when she can no longer "fly." Eva's ex-husband, Tony, accuses her of murdering her first husband and making it look like an accident, while Fred's brother, Oz, prefers his interactions with the elephant, which is named Grace Kelly, to interactions with other human beings. The conjoined twins, who never appear during the play, are mysteriously discontented. Norman has openly acknowledged that the play is flawed, telling one interviewer, "*Circus Valentine* is a play about too many people" (Hatcher 192).

Norman once explained the play's plot: "An aging trapeze artist goes up to try a triple somersault in order to save this small circus, falls and dies. Isn't that a cheery plot?" (Brustein 186). Her comment indicates that in its original performance, the play had a different conclusion than it does in its published form, since in the published version Goldie mentions the possibility of attempting the difficult move but does not actually attempt it.

The circus is so financially strapped that Fred still owes Tony, his former brother-in-law, last year's bonus but cannot repay it until the shopping center owner, Reeves, pays him. There is no money left in the safe to buy the needed ninety pounds of horsemeat for the big cats, let alone one hundred pounds of hay, twenty pounds of grain, and twenty pounds of dog food that the circus needs to feed its animals. Fred may not even be able to meet payroll. His own daughter calls him a cheapskate (*CW* 129). He tells his wife that they cannot have a baby because "It could cost a thousand dollars, Goldie, and that would put new tires on all the trucks" (127). Fred eventually reveals that he has promised Reeves he can take the tent under which the circus performs if the circus does not generate at least $1,000 a week. While eventually the audience learns the real reason why the circus has so little money at the moment, it is clear that the show's finances have been precarious for a long time. In that respect, Circus Valentine is typical: "The high physical risks associated with circus performance inside the tent have always been mirrored in the dangers of financial investments in the running of the circuses which may just as well flip between glories and mighty falls. For this reason circuses have never been run by people who already have money and respectability, but rather by opportunists who have neither and therefore have nothing to lose" (Stoddart 49).

Circus Valentine has become shabby around the edges. Eva, the aerialist, derides its attractions as "Mangy ponies, frayed ropes, freaks, fatsos and fortunetellers!" (*CW* 113). Leroy calls Circus Valentine "a two-bit show" and suggests that Trina could do better: "Ringling doesn't use hand-me-down costumes, I bet. I'd like to see you in something that really fit" (131). The circus has an elephant only because Oz took the colicky animal, which had inappropriately been given ice water, after she was abandoned by a petting zoo.

In his role as ringmaster, Fred concludes his opening spiel by celebrating the circus's star attraction: "Brad and Bill Evans. Circus Valentine's very own set of authentic Siamese twins, their inside arms joined fingertip to shoulder, standing and sleeping side by side, walking arm in arm for life. And juggling" (111). Conjoined twins—identical twins physically joined to each other at birth—first became a circus attraction when P. T. Barnum exhibited a pair of such twins from Siam (now Thailand) as freaks in his American Museum in New York. Chang and Eng Bunker (who anglicized their names), were joined at the sternum when they were born in 1811. During their six weeks as an exhibit in the American Museum, they performed acrobatics (Fahy 8), including somersaults and backflips (Orser 28). The power of the spectacle of their conjoined bodies is suggested by the historical use of the term "Siamese twins" to refer to all conjoined twins.

Norman carefully foreshadows the play's emotional climax. Reeves makes clear that "as long as this show had those Siamese twins, we had a deal. But no boys, no deal" (*CW* 116). His demand becomes even more explicit later: "I've told the people that we'll have a circus with Siamese twin clowns and I will have a circus with Siamese twin clowns or I will have no circus" (126). Although Fred tries to argue that the twins are not all that talented, Goldie concedes privately that the twins are what makes this circus distinctive: "Everybody else has everything we have except them. Nobody else has them" (122). After all, "Novelty was essential to the appeal of freak shows" (Fahy 2).

Brad and Bill, the conjoined twins, are obviously unhappy: "They were drinking yesterday. And fighting. And Brad didn't want to play chess and Bill didn't whistle once, all day" (*CW* 121). Trina says, "They just want to go be ordinary" (121). The implication is that they are tired of being objectified, much as the Bunker twins had been: "the twins were always a curiosity or freak of nature, something different, something other, something that could be turned into a profit" (Orser 182). As one scholar asked of the original Siamese twins, "What did it mean that these two 'monsters' could lead such mundane lives, that this spectacle could be so ordinary? Even the most mundane institutions could become monstrous, recognizable but hideously so" (5–6). Jokes suggest the uneasiness they provoked. For example, in a newspaper article, the *Boston Galaxy* posed a series of half-facetious questions about Chang and Eng: "What would happen if one twin killed a man and the other remained wholly innocent? What would a train conductor do if only one twin paid his fare and the other refused? And what if one twin tried to join the Union army and the other the Confederate?" (32).

When Trina later suggests that the twins could make more money by appearing on television, Goldie tells her, "If they were interested in money, they'd be gone already. Besides, that would be like being back in the sideshow. Your daddy rescued them from that a long time ago, and I don't think they want to go back to it, even if it means lots of money" (*CW* 129). When Goldie mentions Fred's own family background—"you forget that you grew up in the sideshow . . . you forget that you're the son of the Fat Lady"—she *"plunges,"* as the stage directions indicate, *"into forbidden territory"* (127). The usually compliant Fred then *"grabs her by the arm"* (127), which suggests that he resented his own mother being treated as a freak and helps explain why he sympathizes with the twins' desire to escape the sideshow. After all, as Thomas Fahy notes, "The freak represented what the audience was not—the Other, someone excluded from mainstream society for being different" (2).

The twin clowns are not the only ones who "just want to be ordinary." For example, Goldie mocks Trina's desire for normalcy: "If being normal were any fun, people wouldn't be so happy to see the circus" (*CW* 129). Eva later makes the same point to Tony, asserting that he looks down on circus people because they are not smart enough for him: "You had your straight-A life and you ran off with the circus" (133). Norman constructs circus life as exceptional and irresistibly attractive, the opposite of ordinary.

The performers are stunned when they realize the extent to which Fred is responsible for the destruction of the circus that is their livelihood. At the end of the play's first act, they learn from Oz that the twins are in the hospital to have an operation that will separate them. But it is not until well into the play's second act that they gradually realize the part Fred has played. As Tony concludes, finally putting together all of the clues, "It was your idea. You found the surgeon. You told the twins about it and brought them up here for the consultation. You scheduled the surgery and booked us into this town. You checked them into the hospital this morning and you took every penny any of us has in the world and you paid the doctors' fee" (156).

In what is perhaps the least convincing moment of the play, Eva, Oz, and Goldie quickly rally to support Fred's decision even though they recognize what it will cost them. For a few moments the characters all consider how the show might go on without a tent, but Goldie quickly realizes the impossibility: "It is the end" (158). Tony makes clear that what has happened to Circus Valentine is not an isolated incident but rather part of a larger cultural change: "Damn television. Damn Ringling and spaceships. Damn electric corn poppers and Wild Kingdom and zoos and damn me. It's alright about the twins, Freddie. I just wish it was 1910" (*CW* 158). The performers' abrupt acquiescence to Fred's high-handed, unilateral decision signals their recognition that the circus (simultaneously Circus Valentine and the circus as an art form) is no longer in decline but has become defunct.

Kate Stout has called *Circus Valentine* "the least worthy of Norman's plays": "Not exactly a flop, it is still very much the 'poor relation' in the family of Norman's work" (32). Unlike her other early plays, it has received almost no scholarly attention. In a 1988 interview, Norman told Esther Harriott, "I think it doesn't quite work, but it has good stuff in it" (160). Norman blamed its failure on what she calls "premature collaboration," saying, "I got too much help in the process, and it never really had a chance" (Brustein 186). Julie Crutcher, a former literary manager for the Actors Theatre of Louisville, suggests that the original production of the play suffered when its director, Jon Jory, fired the director of another play at that year's Humana Festival, Beth Henley's *Crimes of the Heart,* and took over its direction himself, leaving Norman feeling abandoned and angry (Ullom 61). But Norman herself has said that after *Circus Valentine,* "Then ensued one of those great theatrical fights—Jon and I didn't speak for four or five years—followed by a wonderful theatrical reconciliation. Now we're fast friends" (Savran 182).

Despite her disappointment with its reception, however, Norman quoted the play extensively in her talk at Kenyon College, originally written for the Bingham Distinguished Lecture Series in 1986, and she included both *Circus Valentine* and the text of that speech in her *Collected Works.* The critical verdict on the play understandably still rankles. As she herself has said, "I know that all the plays I write are important, whether they are received well or not. That they are all a part of a body of work, which can only be evaluated at the end of the production of the complete work, not after the opening of any single production" (*CW* 408).

"Intelligence Is Not Always Useful"
Traveler in the Dark

In *Traveler in the Dark,* a melancholy philosophical drama, a cancer surgeon named Sam Carter takes his wife, Glory, and their twelve-year-old son, Stephen, home to his father's house for the funeral of Mavis, a beloved family friend and his trusted head nurse. Sam's father, Everett Carter, is an evangelical preacher who will conduct the funeral ceremony. Sam's mother died when he was young, and Everett believes Sam became a surgeon so that he could save others when he could not save her. Sam admits to Stephen that he took his mother's death very hard: "I was awful. I took it, well, like it happened to me instead of to her. I wouldn't eat. I broke things" (*Traveler* 8). So Sam is particularly stricken that he was unable to save Mavis. He tries to blame her for her own death because, he says, she waited too long before having her health checked. But it is clear that he holds himself responsible for her death: "I did the operation. She died" (6).

His wife, Glory, is more concerned about her son's grief after this first encounter with loss. Exploring his father's childhood home, Stephen discovers a cache of books, all nursery rhymes and fairy tales, and each one he describes has a symbolic meaning. When he recites "Humpty Dumpty," Glory explains to him that "there are some things that once they happen they can't be fixed," much as Mavis's illness could not be cured (6). Later Stephen tells his father that "Sleeping Beauty's father was a fool" because he did not remember to invite the thirteenth fairy to his daughter's party. Sam responds with inappropriate anger: "He forgot because he didn't want to remember! He didn't want her to come to the party! The *last* person you want at that party is that thirteenth fairy. So you just hope she doesn't show up because you know if she does show up, there isn't a damn thing you can do about it" (16). Sam later tells Glory, "You don't invite her to the party because you don't want her to come, but she comes anyway, because she lives there, just like you do. But you forgot, didn't you?" (51). Sam overreacts because in his overconfidence in his own abilities, he never anticipated that he might not be able to save Mavis.

Sam has always had great confidence in his own intellect: "With the exception of a mother who died and left me with the preacher, a mind is all I ever had" (24). He is arrogant, believing that he can save Mavis without difficulty, assuming he will be enough to make up for Stephen's missing his mother, looking down on the neighbors he knew growing up. He is so relentlessly self-centered that one critic has made a persuasive case that he is a narcissist: "His narcissism grows out of having been 'abandoned' by his mother's death, and his response to being rejected a second time, this time by Mavis, is to behave just like a child. He wants to leave his wife, Glory, before she has a chance to reject and abandon him as his mother and Mavis have" (Hinson 114).

Although Sam does say he wants a divorce, Glory puts him off, and he eventually recants. She understands him better than he understands himself. So the audience is primed to believe her when she insists to Stephen that his father does not really know whether what he is saying about God is true and that other people believe and are better for it. She later tells Sam, "I've already got a God, Sam. And I see him all the time, everywhere I go. And He may seem limited and primitive to you, but the dances are fun and the songs are sweet, and every day is holy day" (*Traveler* 50).

Unlike Glory, Sam rejects all supernatural explanations of events. When Stephen discovers a book of illustrated Bible stories and asks about Jonah and the whale, his grandfather tells him, "It means you can't run away from God, Stephen," and Sam, annoyed, snaps, "No, Stephen, it means you shouldn't go to sea in too small a boat" (21). He tries to dissuade Stephen from reading fantastical literature, recommending instead *Call of the Wild, Lord of the Flies,* and stories of the Donner Pass—stories of what Tennyson described as "Nature red in tooth and claw" (stanza 56, line 15). When Everett impressed Mavis with his magic tricks, Sam insisted that his father show him the same tricks—and quickly saw through his father's sleight of hand. As Stephen tells his father, "You spoiled it" (*Traveler* 37). Sam later claims to have spent much of his life dispelling the lies others have told his son: "No, Stephen, there is no Santa Claus. No, Stephen, when you die, you do not go to heaven. No, Stephen, people won't like you better because you're smart, they'll be afraid of you because you're smart. No, Stephen, love is not forever, and God is not good.

And tomorrow is not another day. Tomorrow is this day all over again" (26).

So Sam is predictably furious when Everett tells Stephen that Mavis is going to heaven, telling his father, "There is no hell. There is no heaven. Life is summer camp and death is lights out. It's all just over, Dad. Time's up. The end. You lose" (20). Sam prefers to rely on his own intelligence rather than faith. He is initially confident that Stephen's intelligence will help him, too: "You're a real smart boy, and you'll just think your way through it. Just like any other problem. And you'll make your decision" (34). Only in the second act does Sam acknowledge that intelligence is the wrong tool for making that decision.

Sam concedes that intelligence did not help the Donner Party: "Other people get caught in blizzards and have to eat their families, not me. I'm smart" (38). The Donner Party was a group of pioneers whose wagon train was trapped in the Sierra Nevada by snowfall in the winter of 1846–47 and who infamously resorted to cannibalism to survive ("Donner Memorial"). As the discussion of the Donner Party suggests, Norman is not particularly sanguine about the usefulness of intellect—an attitude she believes has influenced the play's somewhat problematic reception: "I think the play makes people mad. It makes critics mad in particular. It suggests that intelligence is not always useful. It challenges the rule of the rational" (Harriott 153). As Sam eventually tells Stephen, "Stephen, there will be days when it doesn't matter that you're smart. When it won't help. When your extraordinary mind is of no use whatsoever. When all it will do is tell you how bad things are" (*Traveler* 39–40).

Glory knows better than to believe in the myth of Sam's self-reliance, reminding him that he has also had his mother, Mavis, and herself. He has always taken the women in his life for granted. Mavis, hopelessly in love with Sam, chose to go to nursing school to stay as near him as possible. As Sam's own father snaps at him, "Can't you take one day of your life to think about Mavis? God knows, you took everything else she had for your own use, but now you're even taking her funeral. *(Pause.)* I'm sure she's happy for you to have it, that's just how she was, but it makes me mad, Sam" (27). Sam himself admits, "I didn't love her, I used her" (51).

In response to Sam's angry accusations, Everett acknowledges that he put his work first and took his wife for granted—and then he draws parallels to his son's life. When Sam asks if Stephen will ever forgive him for divorcing Glory, Everett pointedly asks whether Sam has ever forgiven *him:* "Some of these things are inherited, I think" (45). Sam is angry because he feels his father manipulated him into his childhood faith in God and his preaching, but he also resents his father for sins of which he himself is equally guilty.

Although the adult Sam now insists repeatedly that there is no God, he nevertheless envisions two. One is sadistic and careless of human life. Sam tells

Stephen the biblical story of Abraham and Isaac, but when Everett says that God is testing Abraham by asking him to sacrifice his son, Sam demurs: "The Lord was bored, Stephen. He was just looking for something to do" (30). Later, when Sam invokes the story of Job, he envisions a second deity, a distraught God who is helpless to rescue humankind: "So He watches, but He can't help us. So He weeps. All God can do now is cry" (33). He later plaintively tells his son, "I actually want there to be something out there. I want there to be a God, and I don't want it to be me" (38–39). His attitude resembles Norman's own. As Norman herself told Lillian Hellman in the summer of 1983, "I hated that old religion. I fought it, I rebelled, but now I find myself coming back and wanting there to be things to believe in" ("Articles" 366).

One of the play's most important religious symbols is a geode, an oblong or round rock that is plain on the outside but filled with crystals inside. Kentucky, Norman's home state, is one of the states in which geodes are commonly found. Stephen discovers a drawer full of geodes that had belonged to Sam's mother, Mary, and proposes getting a hammer to crack one open. Sam, alarmed, says "No!" and then adds, "Once you crack them . . . She didn't like to crack them" (*Traveler* 55). He had gathered them up and put them in a drawer after his mother's death, but now when Stephen asks for one, Sam tells his son, "Yes, you can have it. It's . . . your mystery now" (56). Scott Hinson has suggested that "the decision not to cut the geode open simultaneously allows Sam to reverse his decision to operate on Mavis and preserves the symbol of his mother" and that Stephen's discovery of the geode allows Sam "to admit his weakness, his human fallibility" (118–19). While that interpretation certainly does seem to make sense, Sam's use of the word "mystery" invokes one of the word's oldest meanings per *Merriam-Webster's:* "a religious truth that one can know only by revelation and cannot fully understand." When Stephen asks his father what it was like when Mavis died in the operating room, Sam recalls cutting her open and experiencing what he describes as "Forgiveness" (*Traveler* 56). Norman implies that Sam's mystical experience of forgiveness is a religious revelation that he cannot fully understand, no matter how powerful his intellect.

The play's title, an allusion to an obscure verse in the children's song "Twinkle, Twinkle, Little Star," forecasts its denouement:

> As your bright and tiny spark
> Guides the traveler in the dark,
> Though I know not what you are,
> Twinkle, twinkle, little star.

Sam, like all of humankind, is a traveler in the dark, unable to understand intellectually the mystery that is religious faith.

Traveler in the Dark was first produced by Harvard University's American Repertory Theatre in Cambridge, Massachusetts, in February 1984. The production starred Sam Waterston as Sam, Phyllis Somerville as Glory, Hume Cronyn as Everett, and Damion Scheller as Stephen. The play was then produced at Center Theatre Group of Los Angeles in the Mark Taper Forum in 1985. It premiered in New York at the York Theater Company in 1990.

Norman has said of *Traveler in the Dark,* "It has some of the best writing I've ever done" (Harriott 153). The play shows clear connections to her prize-winning high school essay, "Why Do Good Men Suffer?" and her college studies as a philosophy major. Drama critics, however, generally found the play disappointing, too talky and didactic (see, for example, DeVries; Henry, "Blasted Garden"; Kroll, "A Modern Crisis"; and Gussow, "Surgeon's Crisis"). One scholar suggests that it "is less a drama than a debate" (Harriott 143). Norman later said, "I wrote the play to find out whether it was possible to write a sympathetic smart person for the American stage. And, of course, what you do by way of developing a smart person is let them talk, which is heresy in the theater today" (Betsko and Koenig 326). Norman was taken aback by the comparisons reviewers drew to her earlier work: "It was very shocking to me in the reception to *Traveler in the Dark* that, in fact, everything I wrote was now going to be compared to *'night, Mother.* I was surprised at the hostility of critics to the play" (Harriott 154). One of the reviews of the Los Angeles production was so harsh that Norman has said that it caused her to give up writing for four years (*CW* 222).

CHAPTER 4

"Firsthand Knowledge of How Suicides Feel"

'night, Mother

When Norman was abruptly fired from writing the book and lyrics for a musical titled *Orphan Train* (Beattie 294), she seriously considered enrolling at Juilliard to study musical composition (Betsko and Koenig 334). She wrote *'night, Mother* instead: "I was very angry at the theater at the time. I didn't care if anybody ever saw it, ever acted in it, ever produced it. I just had to get this straight for me. I think there's something about blocking out the audience and just straightening something out for a record. It's a good way to write" (Harriott 161).

"You Know That She Is Going to Kill Herself"

'night, Mother is the harrowing story of a mother's increasingly desperate attempt to dissuade her adult daughter from committing suicide. Norman has resisted answering questions about whether she had known anyone personally who committed suicide: "I never wanted to answer that question because I wanted people to continue to think about Jessie, and not about the people in my life, of whom there are several, who have committed suicide. Jessie's story is Jessie's story" (Betsko and Koenig 337). She has since admitted that she has known several people whose children had killed themselves, and in writing the play, she was struggling to understand their decision (Beattie 294). In 1995, in a speech she gave to the Kentucky Arts Council, she spoke more personally about the suicide of Steve Todd, whom Norman met when they both worked as filmmakers in the schools: "And in my sadness over his death, the strangest protest

kept going through my mind, as if I were arguing with him. . . . And eight years later, Steve's death would be one of the suicides I would try to understand by writing *'night, Mother*" (CW 397).

Norman has also acknowledged experiencing depression herself, although she has said she was never suicidal (Southgate). Still, her own experience with depression led her to believe that as a theater artist, she could offer audiences a rarely seen perspective: "We are generally cheated of any firsthand knowledge of how suicides feel. And in a sense that is something of what I think I can contribute as a writer" (Stout 29).

Norman had also found two recent plays about suicide deeply unsatisfying. In Brian Clark's 1978 play *Whose Life Is It Anyway?* (which was made into a 1981 film starring Richard Dreyfuss), a paralyzed young man takes hospital authorities to court to fight for his right to die. Norman complained that there is too little at stake in Clark's drama because after all, a patient can be as mean as he pleases to health-care professionals because he does not particularly care about them or their feelings. She criticized Vaughn McBride's *The Weekend,* a production of the Actors Theatre of Louisville, for mentioning a character's suicide only in the program notes, not onstage: "we're dealing with real people, and this is a real problem, and we don't do this by putting information in the program notes" (Beattie 294). Norman crafted her own play in response to her anger: "We put a person who wants to kill herself in a room with the person most likely to save her—even with someone who loves her—someone who has a claim on her" (294).

Jessie's mother, Thelma, might not seem like a very impressive opponent, but Norman has pointed out that she is stronger than she appears: "Thelma is not weak and sick and old. She has only seemed weak and sick and old so that Jessie would feel useful. Jessie, of course, saw right through that" (Betsko and Koenig 328–29). Norman defended her choice vigorously: "I did not put Jessie up against nobody, you know, a weakling. Mama is not aware of her strength and when you first see Mama, you have no idea that she would be able to fight this battle. But in fact she is the best match Jessie will ever get" (Harriott 156).

The play becomes a gladiatorial contest between two very strong-willed women. In Norman's words, "It might as well be armed warfare" (Betsko and Koenig 328). Mama tries every method at her disposal to persuade her daughter not to go through with her plan. Connie J. Breding has described Thelma's behavior to Jessie as "aggressive verbal assault": "Unable to physically overpower Jessie, Thelma tries every available communication strategy in her maternal repertoire in an attempt to sustain her daughter's life" (78). Mama threatens to call Jessie's brother to come and stop her by force. She attributes Jessie's plan to a missed dose of medicine and proposes calling the doctor or the ambulance, thus explaining her daughter's decision as rooted in physiology rather than free will. She draws on religious tradition and tells Jessie that suicides go to hell. She tries to prevent Jessie from using the gun, towels, and house, insisting that they don't belong to Jessie. She tries to lure Jessie into thinking about her upcoming birthday and thus have hope for the future. She warns Jessie that Jessie's suicide would send a message to her son, Ricky, that "killing is O.K." (*'night, Mother* 25). Mama then attempts to bargain with Jessie, offering to throw out the TV, get a dog, be less needy. If it is depressing news about the world that bothers Jessie, she will cancel the newspaper. She tries to physically block Jessie from leaving the room, and she begs her through the door not to kill herself. Jessie's only answer is a gunshot.

As Jenny S. Spencer points out, "Mama does act out in some form all the practical suggestions for the prevention of suicide: she listens, she attempts to provide alternatives, she offers transfusions of hope, she plays for time, she tries to involve others, she attempts to reduce the pain and to fill the frustrated needs, and she finally tries to block the exit" ("Norman's *'night, Mother*" 371). Yet Mama is ultimately unsuccessful, despite doing everything right. As Norman observed, "What Mama does understand, finally, is that there wasn't anything she could do. And so Jessie does win. Mama certainly loses in the battle to keep her alive, but Mama does gain other things in the course of the evening" (Betsko and Koenig 328).

What exactly does Mama gain? Norman has said that because Jessie shares her intention with Mama, mother and daughter become closer through this confrontation than they have ever been before: "Probably for the first time, Thelma has something that is securely hers, that she does not need for anybody else to understand and would not dare tell anybody. She has a holy object: this evening that they spent together" (Betsko and Koenig 328, 329). Norman elaborated: "Basically, it is a moment when two people are willing to go as far as they can with each other. That doesn't happen very often, and we are lucky if we have two or three moments in our lives when we know that, with this person, we have gone as far as it is possible to go. After a lifetime of missing this daughter, of somehow just living in the same space, they finally had a moment when they actually lived together, when the issues of their lives were standing there with them, in silent witness of their meeting" (329).

The ninety-minute play, which has no intermission to break the tension, is painfully suspenseful. As Norman has told one interviewer, "In *'night, Mother* the way it's structured you know that she is going to kill herself, but you don't believe it. And it's your lack of belief, it's your struggle against this inevitability that somehow creates the drama—because this is the drama that everybody lives with all the time: Am I gonna make it to the end of this?" (Hatcher 189).

The Play's Structure

In describing the structure of the play, Norman has repeatedly noted that *'night, Mother* is written in the form of a sonata (Betsko and Koenig 334). A sonata is a musical composition that is played rather than sung, often written for a solo instrument accompanied by a pianist. While sonatas may have anywhere from two to four movements, Norman has indicated that she constructed her play in the form of a three-movement sonata: "In each of the three movements of *'night, Mother,* you'll see that it builds and then settles down and stops, there's a moment of silence, and then that second movement picks up" (Betsko and Koenig 335). Typically in a three-movement sonata, the first movement would be allegro (a fast-paced working out of a theme), the second movement would be slower paced, and the third movement would return to a faster pace. Norman has outlined how the three-part structure of the sonata applies to *'night, Mother* (Savran 186). The fast-paced first movement would encompass Jessie's preparations for suicide, her announcement to her mother that she plans to kill herself, and her mother's various attempts to talk Jessie out of her plan (*'night, Mother* 1–37), while the quieter second movement would involve Thelma's making of cocoa and their mutual discussion of the past (37–72). The third movement begins with their angry exchange about whether Mama is to blame for Jessie's decision (72–89).

'night, Mother is usually described as an example of naturalistic drama. Naturalism in theater refers to a tradition originating in the late nineteenth century that depicts character as rooted in and completely determined by heredity and social environment. Naturalistic dramas generally offer the audience a realistic study of character in an ordinary setting, focusing on a life-altering conflict. Certainly the conflict between Jessie and Thelma is life altering, and it is played out in an ordinary middle-class home. Jessie's inherited epilepsy and her severely restricted social circle determine not just her character but her decision to kill herself.

Norman has said that the first line of dialogue she wrote for the play was Jessie's line, "We got any old towels?" (6). As soon as she wrote the line, Norman said, she understood that what she was writing was a Requiem Mass, a religious (traditionally Catholic) ritual that celebrates the dead, and she has compared Jessie to an altar boy, gathering the objects needed to perform the rite (Savran 186).

Norman strictly observes the Aristotelian unities in *'night, Mother.* As established by Aristotle in his *Poetics,* the unity of action calls for a play to follow a single action, with few or no subplots, and the unity of place requires that the play have a single setting. The unity of time demands that the action of a play take place within twenty-four hours at most, *'night, Mother* has no subplots, and its action takes place in the near-claustrophobic setting of a middle-class home. All of the play's events occur within a single evening. In fact, Norman emphasizes the unity of time in particular, insisting in her stage directions, "*The time is the present, with action beginning about 8:15. Clocks onstage in the kitchen and on a table in the living room should run throughout the performance and be visible to the audience*" (3). Thus the audience is inescapably aware that time is running out.

Norman has said, "In *'night, Mother,* I got away with writing an argument; by that I mean a philosophical argument. To live or not—to be or not to be. That is the question of *'night, Mother*" (Hatcher 193). She has noted the influence of the Danish existentialist philosopher Kierkegaard on the play (Brustein 189). She sees the theater as the best artistic medium for addressing certain emotionally intense topics: "There is something about the end of *Hamlet*—everybody ends up dead. Movies aren't like this. Nor is television. But there are some times when you lose really big in life, and this is part of what the theater is willing to show. There are just some situations that end up killing everybody. I think that there's something about that kind of boldness, that sort of risk-taking that is natural to theatrical writers" (Hatcher 194).

For Norman, only theater has the power to show the kind of risk-taking that ends in disaster. Ironically, however, Norman has repeatedly said that she sees Jessie's suicide as her victory.

Choosing Autonomy

Twenty-first-century readers are perhaps less likely to see Jessie's suicide as victorious. Accustomed to thinking of depression as a biochemical imbalance readily treatable with a prescription for antidepressants, they are perhaps more likely to agree with Sarah Reuning, who contended that Jessie's suicide could have been prevented if only she had been treated for her severe depression. But Norman is not interested in suicidal depression as a physiological problem of body chemistry—although Thelma does ask Jessie whether she has taken her medicine, whether she is sick, and whether Jessie would like her to call a doctor or an ambulance, suggesting that Thelma could understand (and would perhaps prefer) a physiological explanation for Jessie's suicide. Thelma cannot understand why a "normal" individual such as Jessie, who is neither mentally handicapped nor deranged, would choose death (18).

Norman, however, is primarily interested in the question of whether a rational human being—and Jessie's very specific instructions for what Thelma should do in the aftermath prove beyond a shadow of a doubt that she is highly rational—has the moral right to end her own life. Norman is asking in this play how far an individual's personal autonomy extends. As Elizabeth Stone, writing for *Ms.*, observed of the play, "If there's advocacy, it's not in favor of suicide, but in favor of autonomy" (57).

Jessie repeatedly compares her life to a form of technology, a machine she can turn on or off at will: "I can't do anything either, about my life, to change it, make it better, make me feel better about it. Like it better, make it work. But I can stop it. Shut it down, turn it off like the radio when there's nothing on I want to listen to" (*'night, Mother* 36). Technology is indifferent to those who use it or choose to stop using it: "Mama, I know you used to ride the bus. Riding the bus and it's hot and bumpy and crowded and too noisy and more than anything in the world you want to get off and the only reason in the world you don't get off is it's still fifty blocks from where you're going? Well, I can get off right now if I want to, because even if I ride fifty more years and get off then, it's the same place when I step down to it. Whenever I feel like it, I can get off. As soon as I've had enough, it's my stop. I've had enough" (33).

But Mama firmly rejects this logic: "You think you can just leave whenever you want, like you're watching television here? No, you can't, Jessie" (78). Jessie sees her life in mechanistic terms, but Thelma refuses to accept that argument.

Part of what interests Norman, too, is whether the individual's right to end her own life outweighs the harm that going through with such a decision causes to loved ones. The answer, for Norman, is that individual autonomy reigns supreme. No matter how much Thelma thinks that Jessie belongs to her, Jessie is an independent human being with the right to do what she chooses with her own life—even if what she chooses to do is throw that life away. Thelma insists, "Everything you do has to do with me, Jessie. You can't do anything, wash your face or cut your finger, without doing it to me" (72). In the course of the play, however, Jessie finally compels her mother to recognize her independence through her radical act of separation. Mama acknowledges her daughter's independence only after Jessie's death when Thelma says, immediately after she hears the gunshot, "Forgive me. *(Pause)* I thought you were mine" (89).

As Norman told one interviewer, "To put mother-daughter on stage all by themselves was new. We'd seen father-son on stage for centuries" (Harriott 155). She insisted to Robert Brustein that *'night, Mother* "proves that what happens to women is important, that the mother-daughter relationship is as deserving of attention as father-son" (191). Here she echoes feminist poet and scholar Adrienne Rich, who noted, "This cathexis between mother and daughter—essential, distorted, misused—is the great unwritten story" (225). It is that unwritten story that Norman presents in this drama.

One of the most common reactions to *'night, Mother* is horror at what Jessie has done to Thelma. Stanley Kauffman, for example, complained that "we are watching an act of vengeance" (48). Norman has consistently resisted that interpretation: "My sense of *'night, Mother* is that it is, by my own definitions of these words, a play of nearly total triumph. Jessie is able to get what she feels she needs. That is not a despairing act. It may look despairing from the outside, but it has cost her everything she has. If Jessie says it's worth it, then it is" (Betsko and Koenig 339).

Production History

The play was given a first reading in 1981 at Circle Repertory Company in New York. Norman recalled, "Unlike other producers who balked at the subject matter, Robert Brustein said, 'When can I do this?'" (Craig 171). The first production of *'night, Mother,* with Brustein as artistic director, opened December 1982 at the American Repertory Theatre in Cambridge, Massachusetts. Brustein later said to Norman in an interview, "That was a most remarkable reaction we had—people just sitting there thirty, forty, fifty minutes after the play was over, not wanting to leave the theater, preferring to remain in their seats and talk about it" (Brustein 189).

'night, Mother then moved to the John Golden Theatre on Broadway on March 31, 1983. Norman's husband, Dann Byck, Jr., produced the play on Broadway. In both productions Anne Pitoniak played Thelma, and Kathy Bates played Jessie. Both commercially and critically successful, it ran on Broadway for 380 performances. Frank Rich wrote in his review in the *New York Times* that "it is Marsha Norman's profound achievement that she brings both understanding and dignity to forgotten and tragic American lives."

Norman received the 1983 Pulitzer Prize for Drama for *'night, Mother.* The play also garnered Norman the Susan Smith Blackburn Prize, which is given each year to a woman who has written a play of outstanding quality for the English-speaking theater, and it was the runner-up for the New York Drama Critics' Circle Award for best play. The Broadway production was nominated for four Tony Awards, including best play. Norman later wrote the screenplay when the play was made into a 1986 film starring Anne Bancroft as Thelma and Sissy Spacek as Jessie. Tom Moore, who directed the Broadway play, also directed the film. Bancroft was nominated for a Golden Globe for best actress in a motion picture in the drama category.

Not all the reviews of the Broadway production were laudatory. Writing in *Women and Performance: A Journal of Feminist Theory,* Jill Dolan argued that the play was awarded the Pulitzer as "a form of anti-feminist backlash" (78). She went on to elaborate: "Feminist plays don't necessarily have to be hopeful, or constantly set in the context of a society that oppresses women. But if the criteria we use for determining the feminism evident in a play is 1) what it does to advance the cause of women; 2) what it shows us about our lives; 3) what possibilities it suggests for changing our lives; and 4) what it tells us about how mothers and daughters relate and can relate, *'night, Mother* fails on all counts" (79).

Scholars, including Raynette Halvorsen Smith and Timothy Wiles, have vigorously and convincingly disputed Dolan's unfavorable verdict. More than one feminist critic noted that men and women responded to the play very differently (Spencer, "Norman's *'night, Mother*"; Dolan, *Feminist Spectator*). As Dolan noted, "The production history of Marsha Norman's *'night, Mother* is an excellent case study of the gender-biased politics of reception." (19). Male critics were more dismissive of Thelma, for example, and tended to attribute Jessie's unhappiness to what they perceived as actress Kathy Bates's lack of sexual attractiveness (Dolan 28–31).

'night, Mother has been compared to such distinguished plays as Tennessee Williams's *The Glass Menagerie* because of the damaged and socially isolated daughter (Greiff), Sam Shepard's *True West* because of its treatment of violence and gender (Smith), Samuel Beckett's *Footfalls* because of the centrality of the mother-daughter relationship (Kundert-Gibbs), and Henrik Ibsen's *Ghosts* and *Hedda Gabler* because of a central character's inherited illness and suicide, respectively (Rosefeldt). Norman's play has received extensive critical attention, including studies of the characters' psychology (Jafari; Reuning; Spencer, "Norman's *'night, Mother*"), mother-daughter relationships (Browder, Brown, Burkman, Kintz, and Kundert-Gibbs), the absent father (Greiff; Rosefeldt), the theme of suicide (Drew; McNulty; Wiles), American regionalism (Radavich), realism (Demastes, *Beyond* 125–44), and even the characters' speech patterns (Breding; Piazza). The play was included in the first edition of the *Norton Anthology of Literature by Women*.

'night, Mother was revived on Broadway at the Royale Theatre on November 14, 2004. This production starred Brenda Blethyn (in her Broadway debut) as Thelma and Edie Falco (best known for her cable television roles in *The Sopranos* and *Nurse Jackie*) as Jessie. The production ran for sixty-five performances and closed on January 9, 2005.

Early in 2014, there were press reports that Oprah Winfrey, one of the producers of *The Color Purple* musical on Broadway, was in talks to star as Thelma Cates in Norman's play for her Broadway debut. Six-time Tony Award-winning actress Audra McDonald was reportedly cast to play Jessie. But by March 2015, Winfrey told the *Hollywood Reporter* that she had ultimately decided against the idea: "I'd like something with a happier ending" (Rose).

The play has been translated into many languages. Norman told an audience in 1988, "Already, Jessie and Mama, from *'night, Mother,* speak Spanish, French, German, Swedish, Danish, Finnish, Dutch, Portuguese, Greek, Italian, Polish, Yiddish, Chinese, Japanese, and Afrikaans. And I'm happy for them. But I won't be completely fulfilled until *'night, Mother* is translated into Latin" (*CW* 404).

CHAPTER 5

Vanishing Children

The Fortune Teller

After the theatrical success of *'night, Mother,* Norman was repeatedly approached by publishers about writing a novel. She successfully resisted their appeals until she received a telephone call from Jacqueline Everly, who was then a vice president and director of marketing for Doubleday. Everly sat behind Norman in class at Durrett High School. Norman recalls that, at Everly's urging, she met with Kate Medina, then an editor at Doubleday, and discovered to her own surprise that she did want to write a novel: "I have to confess that when I had my lunch with Kate Medina, I had in my purse a three-page scene based on an idea that I knew was too big for a play. So while I say that I never consciously thought about a novel, here were these three pages of dialogue about a fortune-teller and on the basis of that she gave me a contract to do the book" (Harriott 150). Norman later followed Medina to Random House, and those three pages about young men visiting a fortune teller became part of the book's first chapter.

Norman published her first (and so far, only) novel in 1987: "*The Fortune Teller* began when I was walking on Eighth Avenue in New York, where there are fortunetelling parlors near the theater district. The whole year that *'night, Mother* ran, I would pass those places almost every day. . . . I wanted to say that those people back there behind the curtains are important, what they say is important, what they are capable of we are all capable of" (Sanoff). She later recalled visiting psychics and reading extensively (particularly about the tarot) as research for the book (Harriott 159; Sanoff). She spent two and a half years writing a massive, 980-page typed draft that she then had to cut down to a more reasonable 650 manuscript pages (Harriott 150). A playwright's novel, *The Fortune Teller* is told primarily through dialogue.

Norman particularly enjoyed the authority of being a novelist: "I wanted to be able to write a sentence that said, 'Edith blinked,' and know that Edith, by God, was going to blink every time it came around to it. She was going to blink then, right on cue, no fuss, not a special blink tonight, not a shrug of the shoulder, but a blink" (Harriott 162). As she explained, "You have that luxury in a novel—total control. It's your own little play in your own backyard and you're doing everything" (Harriott 162). She also liked the freedom from the constraints of the theater. She could write about an explosion in a parking lot or a woman crawling through a cave without worrying about how to replicate those events onstage.

Set within a twenty-four-hour period, *The Fortune Teller* is about Fay Morgan, the clairvoyant title character who believes she can help the police find a group of twenty-seven schoolchildren who have mysteriously disappeared from the state fair. Fay is particularly motivated to help when she learns that Beth Wilkins, the five-year-old daughter of her best friend, Gail Wilkins, is among the missing. Although Fay and her lover, police detective Arnie Campbell, work together to try to locate the missing children, the novel is not a conventional mystery. In fact, *The Fortune Teller* is not a novel in the sense that it is not a realistic portrayal of contemporary life; rather, it is a prose romance, as defined by Northrop Frye in his *Anatomy of Criticism* (303–6). Romances typically draw on intense emotion, feature the supernatural (such as premonitions and clairvoyance, in this particular case), and tend toward allegory. As Frye explains, "The romancer does not create 'real people' so much as stylized figures which expand into psychological archetypes" (304). Frye argues that it is unfair to judge romancers by the same criteria as novelists since their project is so very different: "Here we have moved from myth, properly so called, into legend, folk tale, *märchen* [the German word for the fairy tales of the Brothers Grimm], and their literary affiliates and derivatives" (33). He cites Emily Brontë, Herman Melville, Edgar Allan Poe, and Nathaniel Hawthorne as examples of authors of romances.

So when Michiko Kakutani dismissed *The Fortune Teller* as "contrived and heavy-handed" in a review in the *New York Times,* for example, she might have misinterpreted Norman's romance as a work of literary realism. Linda Ginter Brown observed in a 1993 interview with Norman that there had been a shift in Norman's writing to a more mythic approach; Brown singled out *Sarah and Abraham, The Secret Garden,* and *Loving Daniel Boone* for their "fairy-tale quality" ("Update" 171). While Brown did not mention Norman's novel in this context, the central event in *The Fortune Teller,* the disappearance of twenty-seven children from one town, sounds like a (literal) fairy tale about the Pied Piper of Hamelin. In that medieval folktale, later recounted by the Brothers Grimm, a rat catcher hired by a town lures the town's rats away and drowns them in the river. When the town's mayor then refuses to pay him for services rendered, in a retaliatory move the rat catcher lures the town's children away.

Fay's best friend, Gail, compares the abductions to the story of the Pied Piper (*Fortune Teller* 34). The children at the state fair are similarly lured away by a clown named Pickles—later revealed to be Edith Masters (289–90)—who promises they will see a magic show (231, 249). There are even multiple references to mice and rats in the book: mice on the high school hayride where Fay meets her eventual husband (104), mysterious "rodents" scurrying away from Arnie in the cellar of an empty church (67), the rat that frightens the mayor's sons in the cave (260), and the rat or mouse the abducted children claim they saw in the barn (263). Norman is deliberately invoking the folktale to remind readers that her story is a fairy tale, an archetypal romance rather than a work of naturalism such as *'night, Mother.*

Arnie asks Fay to help him find the schoolchildren because he knows personally how powerful her psychic skills are. He first meets her when Jack, Arnie's brother, is brutally murdered. The killer leaves behind a clear palm print in blood, and Arnie consults Fay after seeing "the palm-reading sign in her window" (19). She quickly describes the killer in such specific terms that Arnie realizes that his nephew, Jack's own son, is the murderer.

Fay also foresees her nineteen-year-old daughter, Lizzie, with a young man who wants to take her away forever. As the book's chapter headings (from "1:00 A.M." to "12:00 A.M.") make clear, Norman continues in this book to follow the Aristotelian unities to which she subscribed in her plays: each chapter tells the story of an hour, and the action of the novel takes place within twenty-four hours.

Fay, a divorced single mother, hangs out her shingle as a fortune teller to support herself and her daughter. Her full name, Fay Morgan, suggests Morgan le Fay, the sorceress who is King Arthur's half-sister in Arthurian legend. Her daughter repeatedly tells people that Fay is a gypsy (48, 123, 181). Fay gives tarot card readings, reads palms, entertains party guests with numerology (53), and consults astrological star tables (112). As one reviewer complains, "at times Fay is prophetic, at other times clairvoyant, and once in a while even a mistress of telepathic dominance" (Kirkus).

Norman herself openly acknowledged that Fay is undiscriminating in her fortunetelling methods: "In fact, reading the tea leaves was the only thing Fay had never tried, though she knew if that was all she had to go on, she could probably come up with *something*" (*Fortune Teller* 9). As a teenager, Fay had suppressed her paranormal abilities to be less different and more popular: "It wasn't really a skill, not something she learned or worked hard to be good at. She'd just always had it" (9). She presumably inherited the gift from her equally prescient mother. When Fay had asked her mother whether she knew "what's going to happen to me," her mother replied, "I always have" (113).

Her mother's last act had been a card reading for Fay: "'You have a great gift,' her mother said, 'and you'll start using it soon.' She patted Fay's arm. 'Just be sure to charge a lot of money.' She smiled. 'It's the only way they'll believe you. And don't tell people it's a mystery. Tell them it's a trick. Tell them they could do it. Tell them anybody could do it'" (114).

Interestingly, Norman has said that Fay's mother in the novel—which Norman dedicated to her mother—is based on her own mother, Bertha Connelly Williams. Bertha's reading of the novel initiated "one of the greater splits in our relationship," Norman recalled, because Bertha recognized the incident in which Lizzie receives an umbrella from her mother as a present for her fourth birthday (80–81) as one taken from Norman's own life (Beattie 285). Norman has also said that her mother "had these amazing psychic abilities she wasn't aware of. My mother just simply knew everything. She's quite maddening in that way" (Sanoff).

Norman has said that she "knew from the beginning that the book was about how we inevitably lose our children" (Harriott 151). Although she was not herself a mother at the time, she chose to tell the story from a mother's point of view: "In other words, it's the exact opposite of *'night, Mother,*" she told one interviewer, going on to explain, "I wanted to say how hard it is for mothers to lose their children, in any way—whether they lose them to the better lives that they raise them for, or whether they lose them to people they marry, or whether they lose them in bizarre accidents—or simply to the process of growing up in another generation" (Simmons). As she bluntly expressed it, "We *vanished* from our parents, and our children are going to vanish from us" (Simmons).

Fay is terrified throughout this novel that she is losing her daughter to Paul, whom she persistently refers to as "the Devil," invoking ancient Greek myth. In the *Homeric Hymn to Demeter* (Athanassakis), it is Hades, god of the underworld (and therefore roughly equivalent to the Devil of Christianity) who abducts Demeter's daughter, Persephone, as she is picking flowers. Hades sweeps her away to the underworld, and Persephone's distraught mother appeals to the gods of Olympus, trying to find her daughter. When Zeus tells Demeter that Persephone is now married to Hades, Demeter, goddess of vegetation, creates a famine for humankind in her grief. Zeus is forced to relent, but because Persephone has eaten pomegranate seeds in the underworld, she is permitted to return to her mother for only part of the year, the spring and summer. The myth explains the seasons but also chronicles the mother's loss of the daughter in a patriarchal society.

Fay suggests that Lizzie and Paul fall in love at first sight: "It was all over. All they'd had to do, these two, was see each other" (*Fortune Teller* 16). Lizzie goes with Paul willingly, but (in an echo of the Demeter myth) Fay repeatedly refers to her daughter's disappearance with Paul as a kidnapping: "The girl was gone. Happily gone. Gone off on every girl's kidnap fantasy come true. Somebody will come get me, it goes. Somebody who knows I don't belong here. Somebody who knows what I really want. Somebody who has nothing to do but play with me. Somebody who never says no. Somebody fun" (90–91).

Objectively speaking, Fay's fears for Lizzie are so wildly exaggerated that they become comic: "If she left on the boat with Paul tonight, what would happen? Would the boat sink? Would Lizzie become addicted to some terrible drug? Would she die in childbirth or get bitten by a scorpion and be paralyzed for life? Would he sell her into white slavery in Brazil? Would an anaconda drop down out of the trees and squeeze the breath out of her? What?" (180).

Like Demeter's, Fay's desire to hang on to her daughter is perceived as unreasonable by those around her. Gail, her best friend, tells Fay to "let her go" (130). Arnie does not understand Fay's urgency: "Fay could be such a witch. So the kid went to a concert. Isn't that why Fay paid for all those music lessons all those years, so the girl would go to concerts? Lizzie was ready to leave home. Why didn't Fay, who knew everything else, know that?" (17). When Fay tells him that Lizzie will leave her, Arnie tries manfully to muster some compassion: "'Honey,' he said, as gently as he could, 'she's got to. She's all grown up'" (38). Near the end of the novel, when Paul drops Lizzie off at home, Fay insists that Arnie cannot let Paul get away: "Arnie answered firmly, 'I can't go after him, Fay. All the guy did was leave me a parking space'" (275). Even Lizzie herself tells Fay, "It's not Paul who won't let me leave, it's you" (336).

Norman's novel suggests that the relationship is an intense and ultimately tragic mother-daughter romance: "Fay understood that Lizzie was the one irreplaceable love of her life. That it was a love affair, only there wouldn't be, couldn't be, other lovers to comfort her when Lizzie left. Lizzie loved her as a daughter loves a mother. But, Fay realized, that was never going to be enough" (282). As Norman told an interviewer, "It's hard to be in this unrequited love affair that is parenthood" (Simmons).

Arnie is fully aware that he is second in Fay's affections: "He had thought about marrying her, but he knew he'd never be as important to her as Lizzie was" (*Fortune Teller* 19). When Lizzie as a little girl worried that Fay's relationship with Arnie was "dirty" because they were not married, Fay herself told

Lizzie, "The reason we're not married is I love you more, and I never want anybody to come between us" (142). Arnie is slightly jealous of Fay's devotion to Lizzie: "Would she ever love him the way she loved Lizzie? Would she be this distracted and jumpy if *he* were missing? Probably not" (122). After witnessing Fay's encounter with her godmother, Katherine Swift, Arnie thinks, "This was a love he knew nothing about. This was an ancient, unbreakable bond. . . . This went all the way back to the edge of time, he thought, to the first two women who stood up, walked out of their caves, saw each other, and hugged" (221).

While the myth of Demeter and Persephone is generally seen as a mother-daughter story, it is also possible to see it as the story of one woman at different times in her life: maiden, mother, crone. In Norman's novel, if Lizzie is the maiden and Fay is the mother, Katherine is the crone. Arnie thinks to himself that she "might very well have come from a tree" and observes her "tapping a bony finger on the table," a witch-like image (219). She is repeatedly referred to as "the old woman" (219–21), and she mysteriously finds Fay at the tea shop even though, Fay thinks to herself, "No one could have known she was here" (211). Katherine recalls the "sibylline wise mother-figure" that Frye describes as characteristic of the romance. Arnie aptly notes her resemblance to the High Priestess of the tarot deck: "The High Priestess represents what so many people are afraid of—that there might be uncontrollable currents which influence their lives, secrets which sway their decisions" (223).

Just as Demeter's abduction by pirates suggests that she is not that different from her daughter or younger self, similarly Fay recognizes that Lizzie's attraction to the man she calls the Devil parallels her own attraction to Lizzie's father, Ed: "Lizzie's father wouldn't grow up, either. No wonder Fay was afraid of this boy. When somebody you've lost to once before shows up again, you can't help but be afraid" (101). Just as Lizzie finds Paul irresistible, Fay had been "wild about [Ed]" (90) and therefore easily acquiescent: "'Yes,' she said. It was easy to say, it was all she could say, all she would say for six years" (106).

Lizzie's experience, as envisioned by Fay, also suggests parallels. Like Fay, Lizzie, too, will eventually lose her daughter to the Devil: "When Paul was finished with [Lizzie], his father would hire the lawyers, bribe the judges, and take Katie away. Lizzie would lose her daughter not because Paul wanted to raise the little girl, but just because his father liked to win" (337).

Despite the similarities between Fay and Lizzie, however, Arnie insists on Lizzie's separate identity, which he suggests Fay does not want to acknowledge: "'To know everything you want to know,' he said, 'you'd have to be *her*. That's why she won't tell you. She doesn't want *you* to be her. *She's* her. She's just trying to keep it that way'" (167). When Fay tells Lizzie, "I've given you everything you ever wanted," Lizzie quietly makes the same point Arnie did: "'No, Mom,' Lizzie said over her shoulder. 'You gave me everything *you* ever wanted'" (336).

Fay herself finally acknowledges that she has struggled with separation. She tells Lizzie that motherhood is tough, time-consuming work that leaves a parent with nothing to show for the effort:

> "You feel a little foolish doing all that work," she said, "so you say to yourself, 'I'm doing all this because they're mine.' My children. My husband. Whatever. And that keeps you working. But after a while, you begin to believe it."
>
> "Is that so bad?"
>
> "Well," Fay said, "just about the time you believe they're yours, they leave you." Fay paused. "And you feel betrayed, you feel lied to. Like they made you a promise and didn't keep it." (281)

She concedes that Lizzie never made any such promise: "You only dreamed up this promise business so you wouldn't feel foolish. But in the end you feel foolish anyway, so it didn't work. It only . . . got the job done" (281). She eventually links maternal sacrifice to Christ's: "His sacrifice had backfired, too. . . . Sacrifice made people mad" (66).

And it is clear she *has* sacrificed: "Fay thought about the piano lessons, the dancing lessons, the children's theater, the book clubs, the art camps, summer school, the honors program, the school trips, and the money that had bought it all" (125). She has no money, yet her daughter has had every middle-class advantage that Fay could ill afford.

The Fortune Teller contains a series of reflections on thirteen cards of the tarot deck: Devil, Moon, Wheel, Hanged Man, Fool, Death, Lovers, Temperance, High Priestess, Star, Hermit, King of Coins, and Last Judgment. While playing cards were first invented in the Middle East, tarot cards originated in Renaissance Italy in the mid-fifteenth century. Originally used for playing card games, the tarot cards became associated with divination in eighteenth-century France (Farley 173–74). As Norman accurately explains, "There are seventy-eight cards in a Tarot deck. Four suits of fourteen cards each, Swords, Cups, Coins, and Wands, and twenty-two picture cards called the major arcana, the big mysteries" (*Fortune Teller* 4).

Norman goes on to suggest that only experience can enable a fortune teller to understand the archetypes the cards represent: "Fay's mother told her she could learn these picture cards by associating them with people she knew, but it had taken her nearly forty years to meet them all" (4). In each of her meditations, Fay differentiates between how her clients typically see the card's meaning and what the card signifies to her. Norman suggests through these distinctions that most people cannot interpret their own lives without objective assistance—not because they cannot understand what happens to them but because they do not want to face what they understand. They fool themselves, misread their chances, downplay the risks, and overestimate the likelihood of success.

Norman's trademark humor flashes throughout the book. On the novel's opening page, when Lizzie asks her mother about her gift, Fay tells her, "All I do . . . is tell people who they are." When Lizzie then asks, "Don't they know that?," Fay responds, "They like to get a second opinion" (3).

> But, Fay would say, it doesn't take a genius to know what's going to happen. The same things happen to everybody. Our children grow up and leave us, and our friends die. Our families hurt us, then help us, then hurt us again. We find our work, we lose our selves, and we spend what little time we have wondering where it went.
>
> It takes a genius, Fay would say, to live in spite of what we know; to be, despite our friends and families and our own best efforts, alone (4).

Yet Norman consistently presents Fay's ability to interpret the cards and predict the future with absolute seriousness. Despite the book's humor, she never mocks Fay's prescience. Fay's predictions are almost invariably accurate, sometimes unnervingly so.

Norman also treats the book's central social issue, abortion, in an ethically responsible way. As Arnie tells Fay, "Abortion isn't about facts" (176). Peter Ewing, the mayor, muses, in what seems like the closest indication of Norman's own position on this still controversial issue, "The truth was, he thought, nobody likes to think about it, nobody wants abortion to be necessary. It makes you kind of sick to think about it. And it makes us sad that we don't have enough money or space or time or love for all the children we make, but the fact is, we don't. Better not to have them than have them grow up knowing there really isn't any place for them" (98). He believes politicians cannot really safeguard women: "Only the Supreme Court can ensure the safety of the women of this country. Everybody else is just too human" (98).

Halfway through the novel, Arnie reveals that, as a Catholic, he believes that abortion kills what he calls not a soul but "the threat of a soul" (174). He explains to Fay, "I don't want the women hurt, you understand. I just don't want the babies hurt" (175). Despite his Catholicism, however, he does not oppose contraception. Fay gradually realizes that he speaks about abortion from experience, as he indirectly admits when he tells her that afterward, "We were the sorriest two people I ever knew" (175).

He is not alone in his confession. Among the twenty mothers of kidnapped children, a majority admit having undergone an abortion, some of them more than once, experiencing a total of sixteen abortions among them (189). Vi Ewing reveals that when she was in high school, she not only obtained an abortion but also helped other girls get illegal abortions (145). Norman observes, "A return to the days of illegal abortions would affect every woman at this table" (189).

Norman even manages to joke about what has traditionally been a humorless subject, writing of one of the mothers that "she didn't believe in sin, she only believed in bad luck, but she didn't believe you should have to send your bad luck to college" (187). Fay is later taken aback when Lizzie "brightly" tells her, "Either you get pregnant on purpose, or it's an accident. If it's on purpose, you break out the champagne. If it's an accident, you try to fix it" (282). Fay suggests that perhaps "it's only old people who have trouble with this" (282). Norman implies (not altogether accurately, as it turns out) that increasingly, Americans will see this issue more dispassionately.

The kidnappers, whom the police chief accurately describes as "terrorists" (212), demand forty thousand signatures on a petition demanding that abortion be outlawed in America. It gradually emerges that the villains are Mitch and Edith Masters, whose motive for involvement is the tragic loss of their own seventeen-year-old daughter. Colleen Masters had died fifteen years earlier from hemorrhage as a result of a botched illegal abortion. Edith stole $500 from her employer and gave her stepdaughter the money to obtain the backstreet abortion, and she therefore blames herself for Colleen's death. Ashamed of her own involvement, she let Mitch think the money came from Fay because Colleen visited Fay for a tarot reading before choosing to terminate her pregnancy. Edith persuades Mitch to take his anger out on abortionists and their clinics. They are joined by a shadowy, dangerously violent young man who tells the children he is Cowboy Bob.

The children are gradually returned to their parents, some when Fay's visions reveal their locations, some when their mothers express opposition to abortion, and one when he has an asthma attack. Arnie recovers nine from a barn next to a farmhouse after he is "winged" by Cowboy Bob (258). Two of the abducted children wander off and are found trapped on a cliff accessible only by crawling through a dangerously narrow passage. Gail, who is the only one small enough to make the journey, volunteers to help and crawls through a cave to rescue the mayor's sons, Kerry and Kevin. The symbolism is palpable; even Gail recognizes it: "It occurred to her that babies must feel something like this as they are on their way to being born" (244).

Mitch is struck by the marked resemblance that Beth, Gail's daughter and the last missing child of the twenty-seven who were abducted, bears to his own daughter, Colleen. As Fay tells Edith, "Your husband has found himself a new little daughter and he's planning to keep her!" (290). After Cowboy Bob is killed by a bomb, Arnie trails Mitch, a Korean War hero whose injuries garnered him a Purple Heart and left him in a wheelchair, and discovers Beth. Mitch had given her too much of a sedative to keep her quiet, and she is found dead, a discovery that leads Mitch to shoot himself.

Edith confesses to Fay that a Brazilian banker funded the abduction plot (293), and shortly afterward Fay learns from the radio that a Brazilian businessman has offered a ten-thousand-dollar reward for information leading to the recovery of the three children still missing (296). The police chief identifies Brazilian banker Rafael Soares as the source of the reward. Fay knows Soares as "The King of Coins" in her tarot cards, as well as Paul's father (303).

Even before the revelation that he is the "financial wizard" behind the kidnappings (303), however, he is a menacing figure. Her first morning on his boat, Lizzie sees in the bathroom evidence of his indifference to life: "Little lizard-skin pillboxes, tortoiseshell trays of dusting powder and perfume, ivory bowls filled with sherbet-scented soaps. Indications, Fay noted, of how the endangered species got that way" (64). Rafael avoids St. Martin's, his son reveals, for mysterious reasons having to do with a woman, a revelation that surely implies that the mystery woman was not treated well (100), and he is more amused than alarmed when his son invites Lizzie to join them on their boat for a dalliance while Paul's girlfriend Alyson is traveling in Tibet. The fact that Rafael plays both sides of the kidnapping plot against each other indicates his utter unscrupulousness and vindicates Fay's fears for Lizzie's future at his son Paul's hands.

Like Paul, many of the men in the novel behave childishly. Gail's husband, Marvin, responds to his daughter's kidnapping with inappropriate excitement and then climbs the giant Indian statue marking the Indian Point Shopping Center and must eventually be coaxed down by the police chief. Fay's irresponsible former husband, Ed, is compared to the Fool of the tarot deck because he refuses to grow up (106), and Paul openly tells Lizzie, "I'm not going to grow up" (101). Even the otherwise admirable Arnie is accused of playing in the shower (90). Interestingly, though, the most unsympathetic character in the novel apart from the Masters and Cowboy Bob is the mayor's wife, Vi Ewing, an opportunistic media whore who blithely switches sides on abortion when she thinks it will be to her advantage. Even the endlessly patient Arnie erupts with anger at Vi: "All you care about is your own damn self, and how much attention you can get, and how much hypocritical bullshit you can sling, and how many people will buy it" (320).

If a romance deals primarily in psychological archetypes, this romance offers readers a deeper understanding of the lopsided nature of the mother-daughter bond. Ultimately, virtually every mother that readers come to know in this book loses her daughter: Fay's mother loses Fay to Ed, Fay loses Lizzie to Paul, Lizzie will lose her daughter Katie to Paul in a bitter custody battle, Gail loses Beth to death, and Edith loses Colleen to death.

Norman suggests that the mother's loss of the daughter is inevitable in a patriarchal culture. It is, after all, the patriarchal figure Soares—Paul's literal father and a banker and business tycoon—who funds the plot temporarily separating twenty-seven children from their mothers and permanently separating Beth from Gail. He is also the one who deliberately separates not just Fay and Lizzie, but Lizzie and Katie. Given the significance of fruit in the myth of Demeter and Persephone, it is probably not coincidental that his first name is Rafael, after the archangel whom John Milton describes in *Paradise Lost* as warning Adam and Eve not to eat the fruit of the tree of the knowledge of good and evil. The fact that the mayor—another powerful and implicitly patriarchal figure—has his sons restored to him suggests that perhaps mothers' loss of their daughters is not somehow inherent in the relationship but rather necessitated by a patriarchal culture. Fathers do not lose their sons in the same way women lose their daughters.

The novel was an alternate selection of the Literary Guild. Reviews of *The Fortune Teller* were mixed at best—when they were not downright hostile. (For examples of negative or at least mixed reviews, see W. F. Axton, Michiko Kakutani, Janice Mall, and the notice of the book in *Kirkus Reviews.* See Amy Hempel and Albert E. Wilhelm for more sympathetic reviews.) Scholarly judgment has been equally dismissive. For example, Don B. Wilmeth and Christopher Bigsby describe Norman's book as "a footnote to American literature" (376). *The Fortune Teller* is now out of print.

The *Louisville Courier-Journal* reported in 1989 that Brooksfilm was producing a film of *The Fortune Teller* for TriStar Pictures ("Marsha Norman to Read"). According to the article, Anne Bancroft, who had played Thelma in the film of *'night, Mother,* would star as Fay. Roger Spottiswoode had agreed to direct, with Mel Brooks and Merv Griffin as executive producers. But sadly the movie never materialized.

CHAPTER 6

Rewriting the Western Tradition
The Holdup, Sarah and Abraham, and *Loving Daniel Boone*

In the three plays discussed in this chapter, *The Holdup, Sarah and Abraham,* and *Loving Daniel Boone,* Norman reinvigorates the American Western, the biblical book of Genesis, and the folklore of the American frontier, reexamining our shared cultural past (specifically in these works, the tradition of the outlaw, the Old Testament story of Sarah and Abraham, and the history and legend of a renowned Kentucky pioneer) from a skeptical woman's point of view.

"All the Outlaws Are Dead"
The Holdup

In *The Holdup,* Norman rewrites the American genre of the Western, "feminizing the frontier myth," in the words of one scholar (Wattenberg). According to Norman herself, she was commissioned by Gordon Davidson to write *The Holdup* under a Guggenheim grant (*CW* 163), but Davidson was disappointed with what he saw as the play's silliness (Brown, "Update" 163). Although writing the play was "funny and a lark," Davidson's disappointment made it "a traumatic experience" for Norman (Brown, "Update" 163). The Actors Theatre of Louisville performed *The Holdup* in workshop in 1980. It has since been produced twice, first by the Circle Repertory Company in Saratoga, New York, in 1982 (*CW* 164) and then by the American Conservatory Theatre in San Francisco on April 12, 1983.

Norman wrote *The Holdup* to thank her grandfather for the stories she had heard him tell while she was growing up (Harriott 160). He lived with

Norman's family for the last ten years of his life (Myers). "My grandfather was one of the most gifted storytellers in the world," she recalled. "He grew up in New Mexico where there were all these great stories to be told, things about ranching and wheat-threshing crews and tangles with snakes" (Hatcher 189). The play has a traditional Western setting in the desert in New Mexico, "miles from nowhere and long past sundown" (*Holdup* 4). Its characters are stock figures typical of the genre: the desperado on the run from the law, Tom McCarty, known as the Outlaw; the "hotheaded rancher," Henry Tucker (4); the former dance hall girl, Lily; and the morally innocent teenaged boy who yearns to become a man, Archie Tucker. Even some of the play's plot points are recognizable Western tropes. For example, in the play's opening scene, the Outlaw finds himself compelled to shoot his horse after it becomes lame. An accusation of cowardice ends in a shooting. There is an improvised graveside funeral service with no clergy member to officiate. Ultimately, however, Norman's play does not so much update the Western as dramatize how outmoded and exhausted the genre has become.

The play opens with two monologues—the Outlaw talking to the horse he is putting down and Archie praying to God to save him from a coyote. The neatly parallel speeches suggest that the Outlaw's attitude toward his horse is equivalent to Archie's attitude toward God. Henry makes the same point later, when he tells Archie that stories about people walking on water or being swallowed by a whale are just as fictional as outlaw stories of the Old West. If Archie believes in God, "Henry believes in outlaws" (18). The two belief systems are equally outmoded mythologies, the play implies.

In *West of Everything: The Inner Life of Westerns,* Jane Tompkins notes the centrality of horses to the Western genre: "The abuse of horses is part of a sadomasochistic impulse central to Westerns which aims at successful domination of the emotions, of the fleshly mortal part of the self, and of the material world outside the body" (107). When the Outlaw shoots his horse, he destroys that part of himself "experienced as mortal, the body and its feelings" (109). In his next appearance on stage, the Outlaw has become *"somebody you don't want to fool around with. This man looks dangerous"* (*Holdup* 9). Robert Cooperman suggests that Norman's Outlaw is as much icon as individual: "By defining himself as Billy the Kid and Jesse James, and by using their names almost simultaneously as if he were both at once, the Outlaw proves himself to be a sort of 'Platonic Outlaw,' a man who embodies all the gunslingers of Old West lore and thus a mythic figure himself" (100).

Certainly he fulfills common expectations of the gunslinger. For example, "Westerns are full of contrasts between people who spout words and people who act" (Tompkins 51). When Lily tells the Outlaw, "A girl needs to hear a man talk a little," he asks incredulously, "You want to hear me *talk*?" (*Holdup* 20–21). By contrast, Archie is told by each of the other characters that he talks too much and should shut up (12, 13 58). The Outlaw tells Lily, "I've seen these new people. There's nothing to 'em. All talk" (40). He subscribes to the Western's traditional rejection of language: "The Western hero's silence symbolizes a massive suppression of the inner life . . . [that] exacts its price in the end" (Tompkins 66). For the Outlaw, who has spent twenty years alone after running from the bank robbery in Delta, Colorado, where his accomplices—his brother and nephew—were gruesomely killed, its price is an isolation so profound that he is wistfully fascinated by ordinary family life and, interestingly, *Christian* family life in particular, with its Easter egg hunts and Christmas trees.

The Outlaw's attitude represents one of several departures from the conventions of the genre. Tompkins argues that "the Western deliberately rejects evangelical Protestantism" and accomplishes "the destruction of female authority" (39), but *The Holdup* opens and closes with Archie's earnest prayers to God, and Lily is the most authoritative character in the play. She demonstrates her agency by excoriating the Outlaw for his unnecessary violence, working with Archie to save the Outlaw's life after the morphine overdose, and freely choosing Archie, whom she calls "the first person I have genuinely liked in a long time" (*Holdup* 58), as a sexual partner. Tompkins suggests that perfunctory makeshift funerals signal the traditional Western's dismissiveness towards Christian faith (37, 53), but in the makeshift funeral in Norman's play, which Norman herself has called "a very funny funeral" (Savran 184), Lily and Archie recite the 23rd Psalm in unison—and without apparent irony. It is only the Outlaw who fits the genre's traditional approach by mangling the one inappropriate Bible quote he can remember: "Dust to dust, an eye for a tooth" (*Holdup* 42). The traditional Western's theme of the masculine pursuit of vengeance, Norman implies, literally does not make much sense.

Again and again, Norman depicts an odd sense of belatedness in this work. "Do you know what year this is?" Lily asks the Outlaw (17). The West has transformed during the Outlaw's years as a fugitive. He fails to recognize the equipment used on the farm, so Archie must explain its presence: "It's a brand new separator. Thing threshes ten times as much wheat as the old one in half the time. Gonna change everything" (12). The Outlaw grumbles about its appearance, but Norman implies that he does so to mask how taken aback he is by technology's potential to transform the West. He is not any happier about Lily's "Big black Buick" (15), asking her irritably, "Why the hell did you buy an automobile?" (16). He is stunned when Henry willingly ties up his own brother: "Is this how people do now? Cause if it is, I don't want any part of it. . . . I mean, you drop out of sight for a little while and look what we got for boys now. And you're drivin' a car and talkin' hard, girl" (28). Lily later tells him, "It was the car, wasn't it. If I had come on a horse, none of this would have happened. You just didn't want to ride away in an automobile" (66). Henry, amused by the Outlaw's unwillingness to ride in a car, taunts him: "Is that the holdup, pops?" (22), and the Outlaw responds by asking Archie if he would like to see a holdup. The Outlaw's pun plays on Norman's title, a word meaning both a delay-inducing obstacle and a robbery at gunpoint.

In her study of the Western genre in film and literature, Tompkins notes, "its emphasis on proving manhood requires a technologically primitive environment" (34). In Norman's play, however, the onset of the Great War further emphasizes the way technology is changing the culture. "Some Archduke Somebody-or-other got killed and it's all about to blow up!" Archie tells his brother. "They're gonna fly airplanes in this war, Henry!" (*Holdup* 8). Archie is also the one who tells the Outlaw that it is not fair for him to shoot them: "It's not civilized. We're a state now. It's 1914" (11). The play ends with an unspecified World War I song—perhaps "It's a Long Way to Tipperary"—and the sound of a train whistle, both signals of an encroaching modernity.

Attracted by the advent of modernity, Archie longs to be a railroad engineer: "I could sit there all day, swapping stories with the fireman, check my pressure gauge, watch the sky cloud up, look out back at where we've been, see our smoke . . . Chief Engineer on the Overland Flyer" (59). When he confesses to Lily that he would like to see New York, he mentions that what attracts him about the urban environment is "Crowds. *(She laughs.)* I want to bump into things, people cars." (59). Archie envies Lily when she tells him that on a trip to St. Louis, she saw Teddy Roosevelt flying in an airplane with the Wright Brothers Flying Team.

Robert Cooperman suggests that "*The Holdup* defines the characters in relation to the future" (100). Archie and Lily are both enthusiastic about its possibilities, but the Outlaw is unwilling to change. As he later tells Archie, "Well I'm glad I'm not gonna be there for the future then" (*Holdup* 64). His attempted suicide through a morphine overdose emphasizes how hopelessly out of place he feels in the modern West. As Lily acknowledges, "He wants it to be like it was" (49).

But it is not just the Outlaw who longs to live in the past. Henry daydreams about belonging to a gang and offers to join the Outlaw and blow up safes, hold the gang's horses, or serve as their lookout, but as Archie says prosaically, "All the outlaws are dead, Henry" (27). Lily tells the Outlaw, "they don't play this kind of game even in bars anymore. I see this, all right, but it's when school lets out for recess. Or when we celebrate Frontier Day" (25). For Lily, violence has become primarily childish or nostalgic. When Archie cannot name any outlaws, she tells him, "Nobody knows those names anymore. Just as well, I guess. It wasn't as much fun as we said it was" (52). Even the Outlaw himself deglamorizes the tired predictability of his life: "I've done this over and over for twenty years now. I know how it goes. Somebody wants to kill me so they pull a gun. They yell and scream or they sneak up from the back, it doesn't much matter. It never works. *I* live. They, you, end up dead" (31).

Tompkins notes of the Western, "Often, death makes a sudden, momentary appearance early in the story, as if to put us on notice that life is what is at stake here, and nothing less" (24). Halfway through Norman's play, Henry Tucker accuses the Outlaw of cowardice, angering him, and then dares him to draw. The Outlaw promptly shoots Henry dead (*Holdup* 33). Richard Wattenberg contends that "Henry's worship of violence results in his death" (512). Cooperman suggests that Henry's death is a direct result of his disillusionment with the Western itself: "By challenging the Outlaw, Henry is challenging the myth of the Old West, and because he thinks the Outlaw may not be the real thing—that is, the myth may be false—he realizes that his life, defined by the myth, may be meaningless" (101). Cooperman therefore describes Henry's death as a suicide that resulted from the destruction of his dream. Either way, the Western—which celebrates violence and outlawry—is discredited.

"In a cold fury," Lily responds to Henry's death by telling the Outlaw, "You are disgusting" (*Holdup* 34). It is her *"commanding look"* that compels the Outlaw to dig Henry's grave (37). She calls him "a broken-down gunslinger" and tells him, "We didn't need to see your Wild West Show" (38–39). The Wild West Show was a traveling entertainment, much like a traveling circus, that toured the United States and Europe during the late nineteenth and early twentieth centuries. Organized by former Indian scout Buffalo Bill Cody, the spectacular and wildly popular shows featured trick riding, sharpshooting, and reenactments of battles between cowboys and Indians. By comparing the Outlaw's shooting of Henry to a Wild West Show, Lily implies that it was theatrical rather than real. As one critic has contended, "Norman presents Western savage violence as a self-destructive delusion that can and must be transcended" (Wattenberg 512).

An avatar of a bankrupt ideology, Tom McCarty cannot even trumpet any financial gains from his life as an outlaw. He carries with him a suitcase that the Tuckers assume is full of stolen money, but Lily tells them that instead it contains "old wanted pictures, newspaper articles, books about his friends, books with his name in them" (*Holdup* 30)—the simulacra that are all that remains of his illicit career. He asks Lily to give Western Union a new photograph of himself for future wanted posters. When a disbelieving Archie asks whether he *wants* to get caught, he says no, "But I do want them to know what I look like now. I got my pride" (19). He is more concerned about his public image than he is about his personal safety—probably because his public image is all that he has gained. Archie eventually burns the contents of the suitcase, "metaphorically murder[ing] his savage outlaw identity" (Wattenberg 513).

The desert setting of the play is "the classic Western landscape" because of its harsh emptiness, limitless possibilities, and hostility to human life (Tompkins 74), but in this play the teenaged boy decides to become a man by *leaving* the desert rather than learning to live in its desolate environment. Tompkins argues, "To be a man in the Western is to seem to grow out of the environment, which means to be hard, to be tough, to be unforgiving" (73). But instead Archie categorically rejects the environment and in doing so rejects the necessity of becoming tough, hard, and unforgiving. While a man may need to protect himself, Archie believes "he's supposed to use his brain, not his gun" (*Holdup* 13).

To draw on Norman's own metaphor (8), ultimately she does not so much celebrate the Western as blow it up. Wattenberg plausibly identifies Norman's refusal to subscribe to the myth of the Western as one of the reasons for the negative response of critics (507). Norman calls *The Holdup* her funniest play (Harriott 160), but she has also acknowledged, "It was just creamed in the press for being too funny. Who does she think she is? Neil Simon?" (Brown, "Update" 164). She calls the play a comedy, explaining that "it's a question of how weighty the issue is. Archie, the center of *The Holdup*, is not threatening to kill himself, he's simply threatening to grow up. It's a simple matter of what is at stake" (Savran 184). Norman has acknowledged that she brought together in that play characters that did not really belong together (Hatcher 192) and refuses to have *The Holdup* produced: "This play will not be done, I don't care who wants to do it. I don't want anybody to walk into a theater and have that play be their first experience with my work" (Brustein 186).

But she has also credited her experience with *The Holdup* with teaching her a technique that she needed for her most acclaimed work: "Some plays are exercises. They needed to be written to explore points of craft, but they don't have ultimately to be presented on stage to have great meaning, great significance for you as a writer. *The Hold Up* [*sic*], for example, was the first time I ever tried to close the set. That is to say, as soon as everybody gets onstage nobody can leave, and what happens has to happen because of who these people are. What I learned in *The Hold Up* paid off in *'night, Mother* when Jessie and Mama are onstage together for those ninety minutes and you know nobody is coming" (Brustein 187). As she has succinctly explained, "The critics don't understand that when they attack a play like *The Holdup,* what is at stake, in effect, is *'night, Mother*" (Savran 185).

"Strong Matriarchal Culture Under Siege"
Sarah and Abraham

In *Sarah and Abraham,* a regional acting troupe works with a biblical scholar to improvise a historically responsible play based on the story told in chapters 11 through 25 of the book of Genesis. The unconventional word order of Norman's title—rather than the more traditional phrasing of "Abraham and Sarah"—signals her interest in the relatively neglected Sarah rather than in the patriarch who traditionally is an important figure in three world faiths: Judaism, Christianity, and Islam. Katherine H. Burkman and Claire R. Fried have argued that Norman rewrites the Old Testament story to reclaim the women's roles, especially Sarah's: "Norman's play becomes something of a feminist midrash; that is, a feminist exegesis of the biblical tale of Sarah and Abraham" (130).

Kitty, the play's protagonist, asks skeptically, "Why are we doing a Bible story? People hate the Bible" (*CW* 278). Norman, raised by fundamentalist parents, had long been puzzled by the story in Genesis. "I had always been curious about the story ever since I was a girl. I did not understand this story as told by the Bible. What, what was she doing?" Norman said in an interview (Brown, "Update" 173). Specifically, Norman did not understand Sarah's purpose in sending her husband to impregnate her maid. "I began to read some of the feminist theologians and scholars on this subject and discovered that, in fact, the Bible was simply one version. There was great evidence that Sarah was a personification of strong matriarchal culture under siege," Norman explained. "I've just really found that the story of *Sarah and Abraham* was a kind of way of looking at what had happened to the world—that the world had been taken over by a patriarchal view, and the power had shifted to the patriarchs. That explained a lot of what made me uncomfortable" (173).

As the actors in this regional theater company improvise their own version of the biblical story, they both struggle with the motivations of the biblical characters and reflect on their relevance to the lives of their contemporary counterparts. The Old Testament is clearly unfamiliar material for them; as Jack concedes, "none of us know jack shit about the Bible" (*CW* 279). Yet they gradually discover emotional connections with the ancient figures of the holy text.

Perhaps to keep the play from becoming too stodgy, Norman adds touches of humor throughout. For example, when Kitty/Sarah asks, "How are your sheep?" Abraham/Cliff responds, "Not ba-a-ad" (282). Later Jack/God rants, "I hate ham. It's bad for you. There ought to be a law against it" (305)—a comic reference to the Old Testament's prohibition against eating pork (Leviticus 11:7–8). When Abraham/Cliff somewhat petulantly objects to Jack's decision to cut Abraham's "big scenes" in Sodom and Gomorrah, Jack snaps, "you can do Sodom when you do the movie" (*CW* 308).

Norman has called this drama her "marriage play" (Brown, "Update" 173), but if so, it is an odd designation, for it's really more a "dissolution of marriage play," in which the audience sees the unraveling of the relationship between Sarah/Kitty and Abraham/Cliff as a result of betrayal and infidelity. After all, at the end of the play, Abraham/Cliff travels to New York with the production, while Sarah/Kitty, pregnant, stays home (*CW* 330). Despite the occasional flashes of humor noted earlier, the overall tone of the work is often tense, even bitter: "Although the couple hesitates to confront their marital problems head-on, their improvisations on the biblical text make them come to terms with their rocky relationship" (Innes 273). There are signs of trouble in the marital relationship from the very beginning of the play, when Abraham/Cliff tells Jack that Sarah/Kitty loves the theater and the town and has no desire to leave, and then adds: "And I don't totally hate it here" (*CW* 276). When Jack suggests that Abraham owes Sarah because she brought property to their marriage, Kitty is horrified at the thought of the harm that kind of power imbalance can cause in a relationship: "If he owes me, he hates me" (283). She fails to recognize that her husband feels that their own contemporary relationship is just as imbalanced. Cliff makes the parallels clear when he suggests that Abraham resents Sarah's popularity (just as Cliff resents Kitty's theatrical acclaim):

> ABRAHAM: . . . This is *her* town and he knows it. That's why he wants to get away. They worship her here.
>
> SARAH: He knew that when he married her.
>
> ABRAHAM: Well, maybe he didn't know how tired he'd get, walking up the hill to talk to her. (*CW* 286)

It is telling that Cliff seems unable to imagine that Sarah and Abraham might have had a long-lasting marriage without serious financial or sexual difficulties: "Well, don't you think they're having some money trouble? Or maybe things have gotten real routine in the bed or something" (*CW* 281).

Things come to a head when a confrontation between Sarah and Abraham reveals fault lines in Cliff and Kitty's troubled marriage:

> SARAH: I want our life to stay the way it is.
>
> ABRAHAM: It's already changed. As soon as I started wanting something else, it was over, wasn't it?
>
> SARAH: No, it's not over til [*sic*] you leave me.
>
> ABRAHAM: I'm not leaving you. All Abraham wants to do is move to the coast.

SARAH: Where everybody leaves everybody and nobody gives a shit. (283)

Kitty wants to preserve their marriage, but Cliff insists that the marriage has already changed, perhaps irrevocably. Kitty defines marriage as togetherness—"it's not over til you leave me"—but Cliff continues to pressure her to move. Her sarcastic response invokes memories of a very similar exchange in Ernest Hemingway's "Hills like White Elephants," in which a young man tries to pressure a pregnant young woman to have an abortion:

> "And you think then we'll be all right and be happy."
> "I know we will. You don't have to be afraid. I've known lots of people that have done it."
> "So have I," said the girl. "And afterward they were all so happy." (Hemingway 213)

Norman implies that Cliff is seeking a way to escape the marriage without any emotional fallout afterward. Like Hemingway's young man, Cliff, by pressuring Kitty, wants to achieve his selfish goal—without regard for her feelings and without recognizing that he is destroying the relationship.

Another intense exchange occurs when Sarah/Kitty points out that Abraham/Cliff "fucks" one of her maids until pregnancy results. When Hagar/Monica, the maid in question, snaps, "And whose fault is that?" Sarah/Kitty denies any responsibility and runs out of the room distraught (*CW* 286). Later, when Kitty asks Jack why Sarah cannot have her own extramarital liaison, Jack falls back on the sexual double standard: "It would be horrible. How could we believe in her after that?" (289). Only a few pages later, he reassures Abraham/Cliff that "the audience can forgive you passion" (298). Illicit passion is "forgivable" in men but "horrible" in women.

Kitty is finally confronted with Cliff's infidelity with Monica when she sees their easy physical intimacy in the scene where Abraham first meets Hagar (293). He does not return home for a week (298); they negotiate custody of their cat (318). They even engage in a quick postmortem in which a bewildered Cliff/Abraham asks why this infidelity was so different from "all the other times" (326). Although he has clearly cheated repeatedly, however, there is a strong suggestion that it is Cliff's ambition, not his infidelity, that destroys the marriage. Relegated to small roles—"Hamlet's valet's friend, Romeo's florist" (276)—Cliff longs for fame and professional recognition, the kind of validation Kitty takes for granted.

Kitty's decision to leave the theater to bear a child has been viewed with some skepticism (see, for example, Weales, "Coming Apart" 19). Burkman and Fried suggest that it could be perceived as stereotypically feminine, although they ultimately dismiss that charge, seeing Kitty's decision instead as a sign of her independence and self-determination. As Kari-Anne Innes notes, "The conundrum is that if Sarah chooses to follow her husband's dream to pursue a career in New York, it may be considered 'antifeminist,' whereas if Kitty chooses not to follow her husband, but to stay in regional theatre where she is content to raise a child on her own, it may likewise be considered 'antifeminist'" (Innes 281).

Perhaps the most mysterious character in Norman's play is Virginia Mason, "world famous Bible scholar and soon-to-be playwright from the University of Wisconsin" (*CW* 279). As Innes points out, Virginia is a stand-in for the dramatist: "Marsha Norman may be seen as a counterpart to Virginia" because "she is a 'virgin' to biblical scholarship, or rather, a Pulitzer Prize-winning playwright and 'soon-to-be theologian from New York City'" (258). Innes suggests that the women's goal in the improvisation is to "recuperate the women's voices silenced in the biblical narrative" (283). After all, as one biblical scholar observes, "Though Abraham prevails in scripture as the symbol of faith, his story pivots on two women, Sarah and Hagar, who shape and challenge faith" (Trible 9).

But if the women's goal in participating in the play within the play is ultimately subversive, they must first contend with the utterly conventional stance of the play's director. As reviewers noted with some amusement, Jack, the director of the play within the play, also plays the role of the deity. Jack asks the troupe, "So, what do you think, folks? Should we cast somebody as God and have him walk around like he was really there, or what?" Sarah/Kitty drily responds, "What do we need God for if we've got you?" (*CW* 299). Burkman and Fried describe Jack as "invested in an amusingly clichéd vision of how the drama should work itself out in traditional patriarchal terms on stage" (123–24). Near the very beginning of the play, Jack tells a thrilled Cliff that "you'll be the one we're watching. I mean, who do we remember from this story? Sarah? No. Hagar? No. Abraham. Yes. Abraham the Patriarch" (*CW* 277).

Ironically, as one biblical scholar observes, the Genesis story is not quite as patriarchal as Jack believes. Drawing on the Bible's original name for Abraham, Phyllis Trible writes, "No mighty patriarch is Abram, but rather the silent, acquiescent, and minor figure in a drama between two women" (11).

Despite the energetic collaboration of the actors, director, and playwright, the play within the play is curiously wooden. Even Jack and Abraham complain that the biblical play's language is "stilted" and "stiff" (*CW* 285). As Burkman and Fried observe, "Why the audience is applauding madly and the critic reports his enthusiasm is hard to imagine" (130). Gerald Weales is similarly disenchanted ("Coming Apart" 19).

Anticipating Norman's project, Old Testament scholar Katheryn Pfisterer Darr suggests of the biblical story, "Patriarchal society is the stage upon which our story is played out. And, if we may extend our metaphor a bit, both Sarah and Hagar are actors under the direction—indeed, the total control—of a director: the anonymous, omniscient biblical narrator" (154). Both Kitty and Monica are frustrated with their stereotyped roles. "I'm always the wife," Kitty says. "And I'm always the one with no clothes on," Monica responds (*CW* 280). Ironically, they enact these stereotypes faithfully—until they do not. Kitty, for example, has long tolerated Cliff's affairs (326), and Monica a little bitterly acknowledges that her primary advantage is her sex appeal: "You've got all this wisdom and power, and all I've got is good legs" (303). In that respect, she perhaps resembles Hagar, whose most significant characteristic is her powerlessness. Yet Monica, as a movie star, is hardly powerless. Unlike Hagar, she does not bear a child and does not suffer exile.

Recalling Tammy Wynette's country song "Stand By Your Man" (also referenced in the stage directions in Norman's early play *Third and Oak: The Laundromat*), Jack tells Kitty, "Kitty, who Sarah *really* was is not part of our story here. It's the Bible version we're after. How marriage used to be. You loved this man. *(Indicating Cliff.)* You stood behind him, all the way. When God told him to move, you started packing" (280–81). It is also Jack who expresses concern about the legitimacy of Hagar's son (301)—by definition a patriarchal concern. The conclusion of the biblical story restores power to men over women. As Trible has noted:

> Not surprisingly, the narrated ending continues to undermine Hagar. First, though it restores her name, it silences her voice. Second, it stresses not her motherhood but the fatherhood of Abram, whom the messenger of Yahweh never mentioned. Third, in reporting that Abram names the son Ishmael, it strips Hagar of the power that God gave her [to name her son]. Moreover, the ending undercuts Sarai. The one who spoke of building up herself, not Abram, through Hagar's child receives no mention at all. Neither Hagar nor Sarai but Abram has a son whom he names Ishmael. Patriarchy is well in control. This conclusion to a scene otherwise focused on women resumes Abram's story. (19)

The climax of Norman's play is Abraham's near-sacrifice of his son, Isaac, and the responses to that climactic event divide neatly along gender lines. All three of the women react with horror. First, *"Sarah sees the vengeance in their eyes and runs off screaming,"* and then Hagar *"leaves the stage"* after saying unequivocally, "This is sick" (*CW* 323). Even the usually subdued Virginia tells Abraham, "You've gone way too far here" before she too runs offstage. The men, on the other hand, take the near-homicide in stride. Cliff/Abraham confesses that he *could* have killed the boy. After pushing Cliff to make Abraham's actions scarier, Jack pronounces the scene "Great work" (323). When asked whether he is okay, the young actor playing Isaac responds with a nonchalant "Yeah" (323).

Why are the responses so different? The women are horrified by a man's willingness to inflict deadly violence on a child. Linda Ginter Brown has suggested that Kitty, Monica, and Virginia become "a community of women working together" in *Sarah and Abraham* ("Update" 182). "They couldn't recognize what they had in common while they were competing for the man," Norman told Brown. "But once they stopped that, and there was something else more significant at stake, like the welfare of this little boy, suddenly all those women were on the same team" (182).

Abraham's confession that he *could* have killed Isaac suggests a terrible anger. "You really hate the little rat, don't you," Jack asks Abraham/Cliff (*CW* 321). A later comment from Jack to Kitty helps explain the source of that anger. Jack tries to persuade Kitty to come to New York with the production, and when she turns him down in favor of motherhood, he responds petulantly, "You were who I wanted, not some baby. And you were supposed to choose me. Not some baby" (317). Abraham/Cliff shares that anger, telling Kitty, "You're leaving me for some baby you don't even know!" (326). As Abraham/Cliff draws his knife, Sarah/Kitty tells him that he isn't angry at Isaac/Willie; he's mad at her (323). Norman's clear implication is that men are violently jealous of their own children and willing to kill a child to relieve their anger at the child's mother.

There is a suggestion that after Isaac's near-sacrifice, Sarah/Kitty sees through both Abraham/Cliff and God/Jack, and what she sees makes her even more determined to quit the theatre. When Abraham/Cliff asks her why she won't go to New York with them, Sarah/Kitty responds, "Because Jack is a tyrannical bastard and you are his blind slave . . ." (325). Abraham's easy willingness to sacrifice his own son had long disturbed Norman, who also wrote about this story in her earlier play *Traveler in the Dark*. As she has said in an interview, "I can't get behind any kind of system which says 'I'm going to kill my son' for *whatever* reason!" (Brown, "Update" 175).

The Actors Theatre of Louisville, which commissioned the drama, presented a workshop of the play in its 1988 Humana Festival, and it was then produced in 1992 by the George Street Playhouse in New Brunswick, New Jersey. Don B. Wilmeth and Christopher Bigsby note that Norman excluded critics from the workshop production (376). Reviews of the New Brunswick production were largely negative. Writing for the *New York Times,* Alvin Klein described it as an unsuccessful experiment on the part of the dramatist, while

Gerald Weales singled out the script as the source of the problem (19). In a 1993 interview Norman said that *Sarah and Abraham* was headed to Broadway, and Cybill Shepherd had agreed to play Sarah (Brown, "Update" 191). Sadly, the Broadway production never materialized.

Redefining Heroism

Loving Daniel Boone

Loving Daniel Boone is a charming romantic comedy set in frontier Kentucky in 1778, during the Revolutionary War. It retells a series of historical events, including the Shawnee chief Blackfish's capture of Daniel Boone in February, Boone's escape from captivity and return to Fort Boonesborough in June, the Shawnees' siege of Boonesborough in September, and Boone's subsequent trial for treason. Also historically accurate is the brisk summary by one of the characters, Mr. Wilson, of Boone's later life, including his return to his family in North Carolina, his later financial difficulties, his flight to Missouri, and his disputed final resting place.

As Norman reveals in her introduction to the published play, the Kentucky Historical Commission asked Norman to write a play commemorating some aspect of the state's history for the 1992 bicentennial of Kentucky's statehood. The commission was funded by a grant from the Honorable Order of Kentucky Colonels, a nonprofit philanthropic organization established to promote Kentucky and its citizens ("Kentucky Colonels"). Only the sitting governor of the Commonwealth of Kentucky has the power to appoint Kentucky Colonels, and those honored include athletes, entertainers, business leaders, journalists, and former presidents (Kentucky Colonels website).

Norman chose to write about Daniel Boone because of her own avid interest in the folk hero: "The Boone believers, like me, make regular pilgrimages to Boonesboro, buy tiny buckskins and toy long rifles for our children, and fantasize about meeting a modern man who is Boone's equal" (*CW* 332). Flo, the play's protagonist, shares her creator's admiration for the folk hero. Part of what attracts Flo to Boone is the soul-crushing inadequacy of her own present-day life. She has a dead-end job as a night cleaning woman at a historical museum. She barely interacts with her coworkers; she tells the curator, Mr. Wilson, "You were the only one I ever talked to really" (354). Rick, the man she calls her boyfriend, has concealed from her the fact that he is already married. Her self-esteem nonexistent, Flo confesses to Hilly, another employee, that she doesn't bring a lunch to work because she eats leftovers out of the communal refrigerator: "There's always something . . . nobody wants" (356). When her gay boss, following the advice of his therapist, decides to try and date women, the first woman he approaches is Flo, and she is infuriated by the condescending assumptions that underlie his clumsy, half-hearted invitation to dinner: "I probably wouldn't even care if we ever had sex. I probably don't even like it. I'd just be so flattered that somebody from upstairs noticed me" (354).

Flo's social isolation and accompanying depression rival Jessie's in *'night, Mother.* It is her extreme isolation that enables her to enter the past in the first place: "The first night I did it, I was just standing there in the museum feeling like there was nobody in the whole world I wanted to see. Nobody I wanted to call. And nobody I wanted to call me" (384). As Flo tells Hilly, "Everybody I see *here* is dead. Dead people walkin' the streets. Dead people askin' me how I am. If I have to spend my life with dead people, I'd rather be back there, where the dead people did things" (342). In Flo's singularly unappealing vision of a contemporary world, she is surrounded by people who are so lifeless they might as well be dead.

Even those in the contemporary world who still aspire to greatness have few options, however, for heroism has become impossible in the present. When Hilly tells Flo, "There's not a man alive who wouldn't go save his daughter from the Indians," Flo responds, "What Indians?" (339). Hilly answers defensively, "It's not my fault there aren't any Indians to save my daughter from. Daniel Boone chased them all away" (339). As Norman writes in her introduction, "it must be very hard to be a hero today, without heroic paths to walk, or heroic battles to fight" (332). She has said in an interview, "In other words, it's hard for men not to be in an age of heroes, and it's hard for women to welcome them when they are not heroes because we've all bought this thing about the heroes . . . . I think what we have to do in order to love the men who are around now is to redefine heroism" (Brown, "Update" 183). She begins that project in this play. "Fixin' a guy's transmission isn't exactly a heroic act," Rick concedes to Flo, who counters, "It is if it's really fixed" (*CW* 381).

Norman both mythologizes and demythologizes Daniel Boone. She depicts him as brave, intelligent, and irresistibly sexually attractive. But she also suggests that much of what we think we know about Boone is false. The museum's mendacious exhibits contain spurious artifacts and celebrate stories that historians know are not factually accurate. Most notable is the Boone Tree, inscribed with the message, "D. BOONE KILL A BAR. 1803. ZOIS" (332). As Mr. Wilson points out, Daniel Boone could not have carved his name on a tree in Kentucky in 1803 because he was in Missouri at that time. Besides, Boone knew how to use past tense correctly, as evidenced in the letters he wrote. Mr. Wilson also says that the hunting shirt that the museum displays is too small to have fit a man as large as Boone was known to have been—although his logic here ironically seems more influenced by the size of Fess Parker, the six-foot-six actor who played the lead in the long-running NBC television series *Daniel Boone,* which ran from 1964 to 1970, than by what we know about Boone himself, who was considerably shorter and less fit (FitzGerald 283). The only genuine artifacts in the museum include an unglamorous ember carrier, a plaster cast of Boone's skull (made after his death), and miscellaneous legal documents. Norman implies that the Boone Kentuckians know and love is not real.

And even Norman conceded that Boone "was really a guy that didn't want to be at home" (Brown, "Update" 183). As she put it, "It would've been nice to meet him on the path, but you wouldn't have wanted to be involved in anything long-term with him" (183). Boone biographer John Mack Faragher has called him "a man of contradictions" (362), elaborating, "What makes Boone significant and worthy of historical attention, even commemoration, is that he stands for some of the things that Americans feel are most important about themselves—the central significance of the frontier in their history, a fantasy of wanderlust yet a commitment to family, a love and admiration of nature coupled with an almost desperate desire for development and material advancement" (351). Norman's Boone is more romantically attractive in imagination than he would be in person.

The play premiered as *D. Boone* at the sixteenth annual Humana Festival of New Plays at the Actors Theatre of Louisville on February 27, 1992. Norman has said that *Loving Daniel Boone* is her "most personal play" because it accurately reflected her observations about American society in 1992 (Brown, "Update" 185). Annalisa Brugnoli suggests that the play suffers from serious flaws in character development: "For instance, all male characters in *Loving Daniel* are in love with Flo, the only exceptions being Mr. Wilson, the homosexual curator of the museum, and the Indian chief Blackfish, who doesn't know her. Two-dimensional as they are, all the figures in the play immediately recognize Flo's outstanding depth somehow. Without doing anything extraordinary, Flo is constantly perceived as extraordinary. *Loving Daniel Boone* looks more like a feminist empowerment fantasy than like a humorous comedy at times" (Brugnoli 236). But William Mootz's review for the *Louisville Courier-Journal* was largely positive, his chief concern being that the second act was markedly stronger than the first *("D. Boone")*.

In her essay on the play, Marya Bednerik suggests that by inserting Flo into Boone's saga, Norman is writing Flo—and thus, Norman herself and by extension all women—into American history. Norman also hints that, like Flo and Hilly, we can draw energy and inspiration from the past to enliven an otherwise moribund present, even if—perhaps especially if—the heroes of the past are flawed human beings rather than the oversized, too-good-to-be-true paragons of legend.

CHAPTER 7

"I Heard Someone Crying"

The Secret Garden

The Secret Garden was the first musical Norman wrote that was produced onstage, and it succeeded both commercially and critically, garnering her a Tony Award for best book of a musical. Her book and musical lyrics for *The Secret Garden* are based on the beloved 1911 children's novel by Frances Hodgson Burnett. The story focuses on Mary Lennox, a ten-year-old orphan forced to return to live with her uncle in Yorkshire, England, after her parents die in a cholera epidemic in India. There she discovers a sickly young cousin, Colin, and the children work together to restore an abandoned walled garden they discover hidden on the grounds of the manor's estate.

The musical opens with Lily, whom the audience only later learns is Mary's aunt, singing a song about flowers. Given all the associations between women and flowers in this work, it might reasonably be assumed that the secret garden of the title symbolizes Mary. But it also symbolizes Colin, especially when Mary tells him, "It's been locked up out there, just like you've been locked up in here, for ten years" (*Secret Garden* 94). The play's iconography—white lace dresses, the Victorian dollhouse, floral imagery associated with women, the secret garden itself—like the musical as a whole, is richly sentimental, making it seem an odd choice for a playwright who acknowledged that she was generally seen as, in her words, the "queen of tragedy" (Mootz, "Marsha Norman Is Back" I-1).

Norman first became involved with the project when she called Heidi Landesman, who had been both scenic designer and costume designer for the Broadway production of *'night, Mother* and scenic designer for the American Repertory Theatre production of *Traveler in the Dark,* to ask about the possibility of working on another project together. Landesman had coproduced the 1985 Broadway musical *Big River,* adapted from the 1885 Mark Twain novel *The Adventures of Huckleberry Finn,* and the 1987 Stephen Sondheim musical *Into the Woods,* as well as designing both shows' sets, and she was looking for her next project. Landesman, who eventually became coproducer of *The Secret Garden* (with her husband, Rocco) as well as its set designer, sent Norman a package containing a copy of Burnett's novel and a British musical adaptation that Landesman heartily disliked. Norman has said that she agreed to join the project even before opening the package (Mootz, "Marsha Norman Is Back" I-1). Working on this musical was Norman's introduction to a new level of collaboration and her first opportunity to work with a largely female creative team. In one interview she said at the time that she would like to spend the rest of her career in musical theater (Barbour G13).

Grammy winner Lucy Simon, sister of the pop singer Carly Simon, became the show's composer after her sister Joanna, arts correspondent for the *MacNeil-Lehrer NewsHour,* interviewed Norman for the television program and suggested that Norman contact Lucy, who had always loved the novel. Theoni V. Aldredge, Tony Award winner for *Annie, Barnum,* and *La Cage Aux Folles,* designed the costumes, and Tharon Musser, Tony Award winner for *Follies, A Chorus Line,* and *Dreamgirls,* designed the show's lighting. One journalist noted that *The Secret Garden* employed more women than the previous three productions of Claire Booth Luce's play *The Women* combined (Barbour G10). Landesman has repeatedly claimed that she simply hired the best people for the job, and the fact that so many were women was coincidental. Norman appreciated the women's lack of competitiveness and their shared interest in making the production as strong as possible, as well as their friendly support for each other when it came to the ordinary problems of family life (Watts 25).

Norman had not read Burnett's book before Landesman sent it to her, and she has sometimes irreverently mocked its fans. As Alessandra Stanley notes of Norman, "the author does a wicked parody of the typical 'Secret Garden' devotee. Widening her eyes and pursing her lips into a Betty Boop moue of enthrallment, she mimics the gasp ('ooooooooohhh'), places her hand over her heart and feelingly whispers, 'That was my favorite book from childhood.' Returning to a sardonic deadpan, she adds, 'That is exactly how they do it'" (Stanley, "Marsha Norman Finds" H5). Landesman has said that she chose Norman for the project precisely because she knew that Norman would fight the sentimentality of Burnett's novel (Stanley H5).

The most notable change from the book to Norman's adaptation for musical theater is a shift to emphasize Mary's centrality as the protagonist: "In *The Secret Garden,* the major thing I did was to keep it Mary's story all the way through, and thank Mary at the end. I mean, Francis Burnett didn't thank Mary. In fact, she kind of lost interest in Mary about halfway through. I think this is a problem for girls, that people lose interest when a sick boy shows up. I was angry about that, and I thought that this ought to be corrected, and I was able to do that. Fortunately, the rules of the theater assisted me in that. You can't change central characters halfway through" (Beattie 293). The shift from Mary to Colin had long bothered many scholars interested in the novel (see, for example, Keyser, Marquis, and Paul).

Norman also greatly enlarged the role of Archibald Craven (he appears only twice in the novel), perhaps for practical reasons: "children's voices can simply not effectively carry a two-and-a-half hour show" (Highland 77). Other changes include an added scene involving a visit from a boarding school headmistress, the deletion of Mrs. Sowerby as a character, and the decreased prominence of the garden itself. Much of the musical's dialogue has been taken verbatim from the novel.

Interestingly, language is an important theme in the play—perhaps more important than in the novel. In the Prologue, Norman emphasizes the exoticism of colonial India with the presence of a fakir chanting in an unidentified foreign language. Mary eventually draws on this same foreign language to construct a magical charm to enable Colin's recovery, thus invoking language's power to heal. Mary also learns Dickon's Yorkshire dialect to communicate with the robin, which suggests that the lower-class Yorkshire dialect is somehow closer to nature than the cultured British dialect she and the Cravens typically employ.

The song "There's a Girl" particularly emphasizes Mary's emotional isolation: "There's a girl whom no one sees / There's a girl who sleeps alone" (*Secret Garden* 7). Obsessed as they are with their tragic losses, it is perhaps natural that when she and Archibald hear Colin crying in the night, they both initially assume they are hearing the voice of the dead—for Mary, her mother or father, and for Archibald, his late wife, Lily. As the stage directions indicate of Archibald, *"Death is a subject he cannot resist"* (27).

As that line would suggest, Norman invokes the Gothic tradition throughout the musical. Gothic literature, which originated in the eighteenth century, is a subgenre of literature that traditionally evokes horror and fear. Examples of Gothic fiction include such well-known literary works as Mary Shelley's *Frankenstein* (1818), Robert Louis Stevenson's *Strange Case of Doctor Jekyll and Mr. Hyde* (1886), Bram Stoker's *Dracula* (1897), and Henry James's *The Turn of the Screw* (1898), as well as the short stories of Edgar Allan Poe. In Norman's book for *The Secret Garden,* Major Shelley sympathetically describes Mary's chilling plight: "What a nightmare it must have been for the girl. . . . To wander up to bed in the middle of a party, then wake up the next morning with them all dead" (10). Perhaps in part to avoid traumatizing the children in the audience, Norman depicts the deaths of Mary's parents in a highly stylized fashion, showing them playing "Drop the Handkerchief" to symbolize the way in which, one by one, they succumb to cholera. The cholera epidemic had earlier been deemed "unstageable" because the director had categorically refused to show dead bodies on stage (Bixler, "*The Secret Garden* Misread" 107).

Other Gothic touches include the omnipresence of the ghosts and Archibald's open admission that the house is haunted (*Secret Garden* 28). Both Archibald and Colin experience traumatic nightmares (47, 61). Mrs. Medlock's prohibition against "wandering the halls" and repeated references to Archibald Craven's hunchback are reminiscent of such fairy tales as *Bluebeard* and *Beauty and the Beast* (14, 11). And the household is plagued by what is hidden and what is unsaid. As Ben Weatherstaff says, "It's gettin' to be a full-time job, keepin' track of all the secrets around here" (*Secret Garden* 104).

Burnett's biographer, Ann Thwaite, was the first to point out that in *The Secret Garden,* Burnett alludes to another well-known gothic work, Charlotte Brontë's 1847 novel *Jane Eyre* (220–21), allusions later discussed in more detail by Phyllis Bixler ("Gardens" 217–19). Anna Krugovoy Silver and Susan E. James have traced further allusions to Emily Brontë's 1847 novel *Wuthering Heights* in Burnett's novel. Similarly, Norman, who was interested enough in *Wuthering Heights* in 1998 to consider writing a contemporary musical version of Brontë's novel (Southgate), repeatedly invokes the Brontës in *The Secret Garden*—so much so, in fact, that one critic compared the touring production to *Wuthering Heights* (Weeks). When Mary asks about the ugliness she sees, Mrs. Medlock tells her, "It's the moor. Miles and miles of wild land that nothing grows on but heather and gorse and broom, and nothing lives on but wild ponies and sheep" (*Secret Garden* 12). When Mary asks, "What is that awful howling sound?," Mrs. Medlock identifies it as the wind: "They call it wuthering, that sound" (12). When Martha later sees the beauty in the rugged Yorkshire moors, the landscape symbolizes the rich possibilities for beauty in what might seem an inhospitable place.Archibald describes Lily and Rose running across the moors as children, much as Cathy and Heathcliff did in *Wuthering Heights.* Martha, the housemaid, and Dickon, her brother, both speak with a broad Yorkshire accent that recalls the heavy accents of the servants in *Wuthering Heights.*

The haunting song "I Heard Someone Crying" recalls the heroine of *Jane Eyre* hearing the first Mrs. Rochester's cries during the night at Thornfield Hall. References to boarding school, a governess and even the heat of India—which Jane Eyre suspects would kill her prematurely if she marries St. John Rivers and travels there as a missionary (Brontë 364)—might also remind the reader of Charlotte Brontë's novel. Even the terrible storm at the center of the musical is reminiscent of the storm that splits a chestnut tree in half in *Jane Eyre* (225, 243).

In the novel, Jane Eyre tells Mr. Rochester that, unlike the lovers in the song he sings to her, she has no intention of dying with him and rejects the gruesome Hindu tradition of suttee (240), also spelled "sati," in which a widow chooses to commit suicide by flinging herself onto her husband's burning funeral pyre. Norman invokes the same tradition obliquely when Lieutenant Wright asks his commanding officer, "Where shall I take the girl, sir? Our orders are to burn anything that might be contaminated" (*Secret Garden* 6). Mary is, after all, very likely contaminated by the deadly cholera: "She was drinkin' the same water they was" (6). Her dolls' house is burned onstage. When she later tells Colin that her parents died of cholera, she acknowledges, "But I don't know what happened to them after that" (59–60). Archibald more subtly invokes suttee, too, when he tells Neville that he hopes Misselthwaite Manor will be struck by lightning (44). Even in that conversation, though, it is clear that Archibald is not devoid of all hope. When Neville says it is not necessary for him to wait for a miracle to cure Colin, Archibald mildly insists, "They have been known to happen" (45).

While all of the musical's principal characters need healing, Colin is perhaps the most obviously ill. Bedridden, he erroneously believes that, like his father, he, too, is developing a hunchback. Mary dissuades him of this belief only by displaying her own "backbone lumps" (92). Neville has convinced Archibald that Colin is so frail that he cannot even be safely visited by his father unless the boy is asleep. When Mary is frightened by Neville Craven's dire warnings that any activity could bring about Colin's death, Martha scoffs: "And what have you done for Colin except get him goin' outside every day, and get him eatin' his food and gettin' him believin' he can get strong again? I think you were just what Colin needed" (113).

Mary's own health has been compromised by her life in India. She herself says of her time there, "I was always ill and tired and it was too hot" (46). She evidently has a sallow complexion, for Martha describes her as "yellow" rather than the expected brown (20). Martha also suggests that Mary has become so pampered by servants in India that she has become unable to take care of herself. Martha gives her a skipping rope to play with to build up her physical strength (23). The conjunction of the names Martha and Mary recalls the Bible story (Luke 10:38–42) in which Martha traditionally represents material work and service to others while Mary represents contemplative thought—highly appropriate for the bustling housemaid and the disaffected young girl, respectively. Not surprisingly, pragmatic Martha recommends endurance as a resistance strategy:

Child, hold on.
It's this day, not you
That's bound to go away. (*Secret Garden* 115)

The musical ratifies the wisdom of Martha's advice.

As Burnett does in the novel, Norman suggests in the musical that poor health is often the result of unresolved grief, and she celebrates the healing capacity of collaborative work. In a neatly parallel pair of sentences, Mary is described by Mrs. Shelley as "a sour young thing" (10), and a page later, Archibald is described by Mrs. Medlock as "a sour young man" (11). They are both haunted by grief for what they have lost. He is repeatedly referred to as crooked and hunchbacked in the original novel (Burnett 8,11,68). Archibald is moved by Mary's request for "a bit of earth" but grants it reluctantly, asking plaintively, "Why can't she ask for a treasure / Something that money can buy / That won't die?" (49). His implicit warning, here, sounds remarkably like that of the Italian major in Ernest Hemingway's short story "In Another Country," who tells the story's unnamed protagonist, "A man must not marry," because "He should not place himself in a position to lose. He should find things he cannot lose" (209). Shortly thereafter he confesses that he has just lost his wife and begins to cry: "I am utterly unable to resign myself" (209). The best way to avoid the pain of grief is to avoid attachments altogether.

Norman quickly makes it clear that Archibald, too, is mired in grief for his late wife. When Mary, bereft, asks her uncle what happens to the dead, he initially responds more or less appropriately: "We bury them. We put their things away, we remember things they said. We . . . talk to them sometimes . . . in our minds, of course" (*Secret Garden* 27, ellipses in original). But then he angrily recalls that he has spent the entire night in the ballroom, dancing with his dead wife, and tells Mary, "They're not gone, you see. Just dead" (27). When she asks whether all those who die become ghosts, Archibald tells her, "They're only a ghost if someone alive is still holding on to them" (28). Almost out of his mind with grief, he cannot let his beloved wife go.

That theme connects this musical to the playwright's earlier work. Bixler notes that "Norman had portrayed the dangers of excessive grief, of inappropriately holding on to the past, in her plays *Third and Oak* (1978), *The Holdup* (1983), and *Traveler in the Dark* (1984) and her novel, *The Fortune Teller* (1987)" ("*Secret Garden* Misread" 106). Several reviewers commented that in writing the book for the musical, she took a sweet children's novel and injected the story with dark Freudian overtones that—in their view—damaged the story's appeal.

The musical was first produced by the Virginia Stage Company in Norfolk in 1989 under the direction of R. J. Cutler, and its disappointing reception prompted changes in the script, set design, and director. Susan H. Schulman joined the musical's creative team as director in the fall of 1990. The musical then had a six-week series of workshops in New York City before eventually opening on April 25, 1991, at the St. James Theatre on Broadway.

The Secret Garden received many negative reviews. Frank Rich ("'Garden'") and David Richards ("Only the Wind") of the *New York Times* were particularly dismissive. Jack Kroll of *Newsweek*, Gerald Weales of *Commonweal*, Miranda Gooding of the *New York Daily News*, Clive Barnes of the *New York Post*, Clifford Ridley of the *Philadelphia Inquirer*, and Dan Hulbert of the *Atlanta Journal* all expressed some level of disappointment with the production. Writing in the *New Yorker*, Mimi Kramer was much more laudatory: "In fact, a good deal about *The Secret Garden* is surprising: It's quiet, charming, subtle, intelligent, and wholly literary in its approach to adaptation. Watching it, you find yourself wondering how anything produced on the commercial stage could be so tasteful, so utterly on the mark, and thinking, Well, of course, they're women" (84). Also positive were Marianne Evett of the *Cleveland Plain Dealer*, Andrew Adler ("Sets Set Tone") of the *Courier Journal* in Norman's hometown of Louisville, Kentucky, and William A. Henry III in *Time*, who called it "the best American musical of the Broadway season" ("Children's Haven"). Scholarly reaction has been more positive. Bixler praises Norman's adaptation as a "creative misreading" of Burnett's novel, and Margaret Mackey, while critical of some of the musical's differences from the novel (specifically Dr. Craven's role as a villain and Mary's physical resemblance to Colin's mother), praised both Norman's use of Yorkshire dialect and Simon's song "Come to the Garden."

Despite the mixed reviews, *The Secret Garden* won three Tony Awards, including best featured actress in a musical and best scenic design, in addition to Norman's win for best book, and was nominated for another four, including best musical, best original score, best featured actress, and best costume design. In a 1993 interview, Norman said that winning the Tony Award for writing the book of the musical *The Secret Garden* was the most meaningful prize she had received: "The Tony is a big public ceremony. The year I won the Pulitzer there was no ceremony at all. I mean, my doorman handed me the check. But the Tony is an overwhelming rush of approval unlike anything I have every felt in my life. . . . It was fun to win the Tony. It still is fun to have won one. I would like to win some more Tonys" (Beattie 295).

A commercial success, the Broadway production ran for 709 performances, closing on January 3, 1993. The show then went on a long road tour across the country. In October 2017 the musical was shortened so that both acts were about two hours and was produced at the Theatre Under the Stars at Hobby Center in Houston, Texas, in the hope that the revival might return to Broadway. Houston critics criticized the show's predictability and "offensive cultural appropriation" in its treatment of the people and culture of colonial India (Groover; Chen).

Norman also adapted her own script into a "Spring Version" that lasts about seventy minutes for productions by children from elementary through high school. Perhaps because of its age-appropriate subject matter, the play is a perennial favorite for teenage thespians. Norman gleefully noted that "it turns out every other high school in America does *Secret Garden* every ten years. So that's send-the-kids-to-college money" (Norman and Margulies 33).

CHAPTER 8

"Sex Just Doesn't Work"

Trudy Blue, 140, and *Last Dance*

In the three mid-career plays discussed in this chapter, Norman expresses a fundamental disenchantment with romantic love. She suggests that trusting sexual passion as a means of self-fulfillment is a mistake, that women need to develop some selfishness in order to rediscover what gives them pleasure and that solitude can be more beneficial for women than bouncing from one fleeting romantic relationship to the next.

"Nobody Ever Lived Happily Ever After"
Trudy Blue

In 1994, shortly after *The Red Shoes,* the Broadway musical she had written, closed after only a handful of performances, Norman became "deathly, deathly ill" (Brown, "More" 199). After a visit to her doctor and a series of diagnostic exams, including X-rays, a CAT scan, and an MRI, "The results came back, and they said, 'This is aggressive lung cancer, and you have two years to live'" (199). Her physician referred her to a pulmonary surgeon, and after another series of diagnostic tests, he told her that, rather than undergo an immediate biopsy, she should take medication for two weeks and return for a follow-up exam. Only at that follow-up exam did she learn that the spot on her lung had been pneumonia rather than lung cancer. "So for two weeks I lived not only with this real debilitating illness but also with a death sentence," Norman said. "It definitely changed my life forever" (199).

She has recalled undergoing one exam (variously described as an MRI or a CAT scan but probably the former) and realizing, "I wasn't nearly attached enough to life" because the only two outcomes she cared about missing were not seeing her son, Angus, grow up and not learning the status of the *Madeline* screenplay, which she was working on at the time and from which she was subsequently fired (199). She knew that that was not enough and that she needed to figure out what would make her happy, and *Trudy Blue* evolved from that initial resolution: "I'm going to sit down and write this and say all the things I'm not supposed to say. I'm going to tell about how marriage rarely makes one happy, that basically we outgrow our men and then have to figure out what the hell to do. We've been so schooled in our lack of entitlement to pleasure that we are living half-lives" (213).

Linda Gitner Brown has suggested that the semiautobiographical *Trudy Blue* is "Marsha Norman's mid-life crisis play," a characterization that Norman herself has rejected (198). Like Norman, Ginger Andrews, the play's protagonist, is first told that she might have lung cancer and then told that she should take a course of antibiotics and return in three weeks (rather than Norman's two) for a follow-up exam to determine whether the spot on her lung is pneumonia or cancer. Unlike Norman, however, Ginger eventually learns that the second diagnosis of pneumonia is a mistake due to an X-ray mix-up: she really does have lung cancer.

Norman has said that she was trying in *Trudy Blue* to capture "the effects of trying to make a decision. What shall I do now? I realize that I'm unhappy. This sort of discussion begins to go on among all of the voices. . . . And this is simply a way of giving shape, a form to those voices" (205). As Norman explains in describing the setting, "The play takes place in one moment, but the events and conversations seen in that moment are drawn from many days, both past and future, and many states of consciousness, waking and non, fictional and non" (*Trudy Blue* 6).

In the play, Ginger is obviously unhappy in her marriage. Her husband, Don, seems utterly conventional. He balances the checkbook and worries about their finances; in a recurring line, he expresses dismay that Ginger has seen seventeen doctors in a single month. He seems genuinely relieved when he learns that the doctor has told Ginger her supposed cancer was pneumonia. Only gradually do he and Ginger reveal the fault lines in their marriage, as, for example, when she accuses him of not liking her friends, or when Don reveals his jealousy of Ginger's relative freedom as a professional writer. Their thirteen-year-old daughter, Beth, mercilessly points out, "The only time you're not fighting is when one of you isn't here" (38).

Ginger's friend Sue suggests that the problem is that Don likes his marriage the way it is, whereas Ginger wants it to be better. Ginger is troubled by their nonexistent sex life and contemplates an affair. She flirts with James, a man who later reveals himself to be an embodiment of her own wishes rather than a real human being. In a line that seems particularly telling in the context of this play about imaginary conversations, James admonishes her, "Ginny, Ginny, the things in your mind are as real as anything else" (60).

Throughout the play, Ginger interacts with other imaginary people as well, including Trudy Blue, "the main character in Ginger's novels," and her deceased mother, Annie (6). Norman has said of Trudy Blue, "She's the person you are speaking to when you talk to yourself" (Gornik). Elsewhere, she has explained the presence of these half-imaginary interlocutors: "In the theater we can present things as they seem, not as they are. In *Trudy Blue,* for example, when I have people who are fantasy figures walking around in between conversations that are actually happening, this is how it is. This is actually what happens. Our world is populated by the people that we dream about and that we fear and not just the ones that we could actually go pinch" (Hatcher 191).

In her interactions with these imaginary figures, Ginger repeatedly anticipates how conversations with her family will go, expresses her apprehension about telling her husband and daughter about her diagnosis of terminal illness, and speculates about how genuine their connections with each other really are. She expresses the anger that she hides from her husband and daughter. She is more open and honest with her imaginary friend than she is with her living, breathing family members.

Linda Ginter Brown has suggested that Ginger's persistent "ear problem" is "a metaphor for the fact that we're not listening to one another" ("More" 206). Certainly Don is oblivious to his wife's illness. Even thirteen-year-old Beth can see that her mother is more gravely ill than the doctors have indicated. Sue, too, tells Ginger, "You don't look right" (*Trudy Blue* 33). Ginger tells Trudy "I just want him to look at me. I just want him to see I'm in trouble here" (66).

When Don reads her latest drafts and discovers that her character Trudy Blue is having an affair, he confronts Ginger, asking her whether he is "Ron," Trudy Blue's husband in her novel, but backs down when Ginger asks him whether he really wants to know whether she is having an affair. Norman implies that he does not really want to know because the knowledge would cause him pain.

In response to critics' complaints that the character of Don was not adequately developed, Norman sardonically countered, "Well, yes, I think that what they're complaining about is that it wasn't about them" (Brown, "More" 206). She later added, "He's certainly every husband I've had" (206). Norman suggests that Ginger's illness is the result of her suppressed anger. Ginger confesses to James that she has experienced rage ever since high school and has "buried" whatever rage she could not use in her work (*Trudy Blue* 36). After telling Don she is terminally ill after all, she erupts furiously: "Sick. I'm sick of you thinking everything is either a nuisance or a joke. I'm sick of sleeping with someone who'd rather be on the sofa. I'm sick of wishing I had it all to do over. I'm sick of memories and call waiting and bank accounts and bargaining with you for the things I need. I want someone to talk to me in a clear, plain way and say what he means. I want to tell the truth without deciding to first" (49).

Trudy accuses Ginger of resisting telling her family of her revised and now terminal diagnosis because "You just don't want them in there where you really live" (52). In an interesting echo of Plato's famous dictum that all poets are liars, Ginger's daughter accuses her of lying for a living, and Ginger later acknowledges that Beth is right: Ginger is emotionally dishonest.

A devoted mother, Ginger is physically affectionate with Beth and repeatedly tries to console her about a failed science fair project. Ginger eventually defends her desire for joy in her life as a way to be a better mother: "I want Beth to see me being happy so she'll know it's all right, so she'll look for happiness too, not just work all the time like I've done. Wouldn't that be the best thing I could possibly do for her? To be happy myself? So she'll know what it looks like?" (32). But later Ginger is less sanguine, telling James, "Nobody ever lived happily ever after. If we had a shred of courage, we'd tell our children the truth" (59).

Beth later says of Ginger, "She wouldn't know fun if it bit her on the ass" (56). Norman has said in an interview that in creating this play, "I decided I wanted to write about pleasure" (Brown, "More" 199), but she is actually preoccupied in this play with Ginger's anhedonia, her inability to take pleasure in what were once pleasurable activities. The playwright is particularly interested in the ways in which a woman sacrifices her own desires for the sake of her family's. As Norman herself has commented, "I think that I'm saying that the things that we've been taught will make us happy don't always end up making us happy" (203).

In the play's emotional climax, Ginger banishes Trudy Blue, telling her, "You were the problem between Don and me!" (*Trudy Blue* 71). When Trudy protests that Ginger is "losing it," Ginger tells Trudy that Trudy is "nothing but my fear of these people that I love" and that she can only connect with them if Trudy is gone (71). Only when she stops anticipating her family's responses can she really communicate with them and pay attention to their actual responses. As the stage directions indicate, "*Ginger becomes aware of Beth in a new way. Without Trudy there, she can actually see her very clearly. Ginger is present, simply and clearly present, perhaps for the first time*" (75).

It might seem, given the salutary effects of banishing Trudy Blue, that Norman is expressing a strong preference here for the value of "real life" over fiction. But when Ginger disparages her work as an excuse to be alone, Trudy insists,

"Your work is who you are, Ginger. It's what justifies your whole life. How would you say what you were doing here if it weren't for your work? It's what you really think, it's what you really cared about. It's your contribution" (54).

Interestingly, the term "Trudy Blue" refers to a color filter used in theatrical lighting. The manufacturer, Rosco Laboratories, Inc., describes "Trudy Blue" on its website as "a rich clean red blue that warms to lavender when dimmed" ("Roscolux"). Norman's theatrical metaphor suggests that, "dimmed" by her terminal diagnosis, Ginger develops into a warmer, more enlightened, more joyful human being than she otherwise might have become.

Trudy Blue was commissioned by the Actors Theatre of Louisville and premiered there on March 19, 1995; the play premiered in New York at the off-Broadway MCC Theater on December 2, 1999. Although it was to have closed on December 18, the theater extended its run until January 9 ("Norman's *Trudy Blue*"). Reviewers were unimpressed (see, for example, Isherwood; Mootz, rev. of *Trudy Blue*; and Simon). *Trudy Blue* was unfavorably compared to *Wit,* Margaret Edson's Pulitzer Prize–winning one-act play about a woman dying of ovarian cancer (see, for example, Isherwood), which also opened in 1995.

Unlike other Norman works, there are multiple published incarnations of *Trudy Blue.* It evolved from a one-act play, *Lunch with Ginger,* that she wrote as an entry for the Ensemble Studio Theatre's One-Act Marathon in 1994. In her introduction to the piece, Norman writes, "Quite simply then, this play exists because people asked me for it. There is some kind of message here, probably the same one that's in the play, which is, it is good if you ask someone for what you want, but it works better if you ask someone who can actually give it to you" (*Lunch* 124). In the five-page play, which Norman indicates would take ten minutes onstage, the protagonist, a woman named Ginger, lunches and converses with a series of three different unnamed friends. Ginger asks how much of our lives is determined by biological imperatives that benefit the species rather than the individual. Her friends, discomfited by the unsettling questions she asks, repeatedly revert to more superficial topics: shopping, celebrity gossip, exercise. Several of the themes apparent in the published version of *Trudy Blue* are apparent here: Ginger has a persistent ear infection that makes communication more difficult and isolates her, and she is openly disenchanted with her marriage.

Lunch with Ginger was published in *EST Marathon 1994: One-Act Plays.* Yet another version of the play was published in *Humana Festival '95: The Complete Plays.* That version begins with a troubling bedroom conversation between Ginger and her husband, Don, in which they seem unable to hear each other—sometimes literally because of Ginger's ear infection (her ear problems are a common theme through all three versions). Their marital discord is much harsher in this version. Don openly ignores her first comment and then mocks her inability to hear him; she angrily tells him, "the first thing you do when we get out to the house is leave," and offers a long list of errands he runs, implying that he is deliberately avoiding her (*Trudy Blue, Humana* 227). In a later argument about a planned dinner with friends Jerry and Sue, Don expresses his resentment of her work much more harshly than he does in the 1996 version: "Isn't it everybody's dream, to make a living by not going to work?" (238). Scene 1 of the 1995 version, "Lunch with Ginger," closely resembles the one-act play *Lunch with Ginger,* first staged in 1994. In conversations with three friends, Maria, Sue, and Connie, Ginger struggles to articulate the tensions she sees between what is good for the species and what is good for the individual.

A later scene shows the audience her yoga practice, in which the shirtless James joins her. Ginger's husband and children repeatedly interrupt her but do not perceive James, leading the audience to conclude that he is perhaps unreal or imaginary—a discovery the audience does not make in the 1996 version until Ginger does, more than three quarters of the way through the play. The swami's instructions become overtly sexual in this scene but do not in the 1996 version. In a very brief Scene 6, Ginger's telephone conversation with an unseen interlocutor suggests that she is actively having an affair rather than just considering the idea, as she does in the 1996 version. The following scene, "Ginger in the Spy Shop," has a much briefer counterpart in the final published version; in this longer, earlier scene, Ginger tries out a lie detection phone in a conversation with James. The implication is that even when they profess to be in love, human beings inevitably lie to each other.

In a brief transition scene titled "Ginger, Her Mom, and Control," Annie criticizes Ginger for repeatedly resorting to wish-fulfillment fantasies. Annie is a much stronger presence in this version than in the 1996 play and is frequently highly critical of her daughter. As Norman has observed, "This is mother as introjection. Here she is—she's dead, and she doesn't go away. She's there still judging and holding her standards" (Brown, "More" 205).

Ginger confesses to a flirtation and then, confusingly, arranges to meet James for the first time before flirting with him over drinks in the following scene until her imaginary dalliance dissolves once again into her fractious home life. James discusses the Platonic idea that humans are always searching for their soul mate, who is the other half of themselves. When Ginger recalls that the last time she was happy was when she was at Lolo Hot Springs in Minnesota, her exasperated friend Sue accuses her of selfishness, a charge emphasized in Scene 12 when Ginger's two children, Beth and Charlie, talk about their mother's abrupt departure from their lives. After a scene in which Ginger imagines a sybaritic existence with James, she calls home and listens to her daughter's anger and hostility over Ginger's five-hour absence. After another tense bedroom conversation with Don, she abruptly flees the house, and her husband, concerned that she might be suicidal, calls her doctor. At "The Book Party" in Scene 16, it is apparent that she is mysteriously "gone," and in the final scene, a topless Ginger joyously emerges from the water in a hot tub in Lolo Springs, Minnesota, saying, "My happiness is in orbit around me like the moon" (*Trudy Blue* [1995] 276).

Interestingly, the final, 1996 version of *Trudy Blue* emphasizes Ginger's maternal identity much more heavily and downplays the possibility of sexual infidelity. Common themes running through all three versions include disenchantment with marriage, the inability of people to communicate with one another or even hear one another properly, and the dissatisfaction and discontent of a woman who has renounced all right to her own happiness in favor of her family's.

The Bitter Pain of Sexual Jealousy

140

In the one-act play *140*, inspired by Shakespeare's Sonnet 140, Norman offers a biting look at infidelity and the impermanence of romantic love. To celebrate the twenty-fifth anniversary of its founding, the Acting Company, a national repertory theater founded in New York City by John Houseman, commissioned the work as one of seven new one-act plays inspired by seven different Shakespearean sonnets. Dramaturge Anne Cattaneo chose the sonnets she felt would be compatible with the style of each playwright. The other distinguished playwrights included in the published book are Eric Bogosian, William Finn, John Guare, Tony Kushner, Ntozake Shange, and Wendy Wasserstein. Director Mark Lamos states in his introduction to the published collection that he found Norman's contribution particularly compelling: "I remember reading it standing up, unable to sit down and relax, as its pages curled sinuously from my fax machine" (xiii).

The collection of seven short plays was produced in association with the Guthrie Theater in Minneapolis and the Barbican Center in London. *Love's Fire* (the name for the collection, taken from Sonnet 154) premiered on January 7, 1998, at the Guthrie Theater Lab in Minneapolis and then toured the country, playing in forty-five American cities before then traveling to the Barbican in London and finally the Joseph Papp Theatre in New York. Reviewers found the production uneven; they particularly praised the hilarity of Tony Kushner's absurdly comic contribution.

Shakespeare wrote 154 sonnets, fourteen-line poems in iambic pentameter (that is, consisting of ten syllables in each line, with the emphasis on every second syllable) with end-rhymes following a typical rhyme scheme of *abab-cdcdefefgg*. Sonnet 140 is one of several sonnets that "confront the arguments that might happen between two lovers and which love in some way resolves" (Edmondson and Wells 69). It has been suggested that "Sonnet 140 could be either Hamlet talking to Ophelia or Ophelia talking to Hamlet; it might be an imagined letter exchanged between the two of them" (Edmondson and Wells 103). The speaker in the poem asks his beloved to tell him that she loves him, even though she does not, and to stop trying his patience with her behavior (which presumably flaunts her infidelity). In despair, he worries he will go mad. In the last six lines of the poem, he threatens that if she will not pretend to be faithful to him, he will "speak ill" of her and ruin her reputation. Shakespeare draws on metaphors of illness, referring to "pain," "fretful sick men," "death," and "physicians" to express the strength of the speaker's emotional distress.

Presumably inspired by Shakespeare's reference in the sonnet to "my pity-wanting pain" (*140* 43), Norman dramatizes the bitter pain of sexual jealousy. Unlike several of the other works in the collection, which have an overtly comic tone, Norman's somber contribution examines sexual infatuation and the anguish of the betrayed romantic partner in a series of short-lived sexual liaisons—what the blurb on the book's back cover aptly terms "a daisy chain of betrayal."

Her piece is frequently described as the most sexually explicit, although that may have more to do with the director's choices than the playwright's, since the stage directions in the published text call for nothing more explicit than *"unbuttoning something, or stepping out of her skirt"* (35). Similarly, Paul Edmondson and Stanley Wells have described her play as "an amusing visual depiction of promiscuity" even though no character in the play has more than two sexual partners (162). The point of the play is not so much promiscuity (which does not seem a particularly fair implicit criticism, anyway) as the interchangeability of the characters. These attachments lack not just permanence but depth.

Letting Go of Youth

Last Dance

In *Last Dance,* a comedy set in the south of France, Charlotte Burns, a forty-something writer, gracefully disengages from her solicitous younger lover, Cabot Gray III, skillfully manipulating him instead into a romantic relationship with her young goddaughter, Georgeanne. Presented with a confession of love from her longtime friend, Randall Dellamar, Charlotte also successfully deflects his romantic attention while retaining him as a friend.

Cab fully recognizes that Charlotte is trying to manipulate him into a sexual relationship with Georgeanne: "You're daring me to seduce her" (*Last Dance* 21). He quickly complies, afterward telling Charlotte angrily, "She's beautiful. Her French is perfect. I had fun walking around with her, being mad at you. We sat outside and laughed and ate and drank till we could barely stand up. It was hopeless. Finally she wanted me so much, I just gave in" (39). Georgeanne offers a significantly different version of events, telling Charlotte, "I know you said you wanted to give Cab to me, but after lunch today, we stopped in his cottage and before I quite knew what was happening, he had all my clothes off and was ravishing me" (42). They seem admirably suited for each other.

It is particularly apt that the actor playing Cab in the play's premiere had recently played Orlando in a production of Shakespeare's *As You Like It* (Finkle), for *Last Dance* is oddly reminiscent of a Shakespearean comedy in which mismatched characters plagued by complicated misunderstandings must be inveigled into aligning with the appropriate romantic partners. For example, in true Shakespearean fashion, Georgeanne leaves Cab a love poem that he initially assumes was left for him by Charlotte (*Last Dance* 19), and then Randall receives an anonymous love poem that he wrongly assumes must be from Cab (46). In *Last Dance* Norman also writes dialogue—particularly Randall's dialogue—in a witty epigrammatic style that recalls the plays of Oscar Wilde or Noel Coward. She is experimenting with a very different comic tone and a lighthearted approach in this work, although its subject matter is ultimately not comic at all.

As the play's elegiac title suggests, Charlotte is renouncing heterosexual romance—thus continuing a theme, one that also runs through *Trudy Blue* and *140*, of disenchantment with the possibilities for happiness that heterosexual romance offers. Aging contributes to Charlotte's resolve. She tells Randall, "I mean to go on . . . alone. I am not scared of getting old, whatever that means, but I don't think it's card games and deck chairs. I think it's years and years I know nothing about yet. All those days I wished I had an extra hour? Well, here they come, all those hours, all lined up, ready to be lived. And if all I have to do to get that time is let go of my youth, I say fine. Whatever comes next, I say Let's have it. I'm not hanging on to my precious youth one more day" (58).

Charlotte herself then tells Georgeanne, "I am tired of love." Later she adds, "I could never have imagined it myself, but I am tired of smiling and being smiled at, watching and being watched. Tired of thinking about it, wondering what may happen, what another mouth will be like, what another tongue may do . . ." (12).

Charlotte's blunt renunciation of romantic love seems almost heretical in modern culture. As Randall says, "You can't be an American and not fall in love. It's our national pastime, not to mention the coin of the realm, the means they use to sell everything they think we ought to have" (14). Her statements are so uncharacteristic that all three of the other characters refuse to believe her, insisting that she must have fallen hopelessly in love with a married French fisherman.

Later, however, Randall seems to share Charlotte's disenchantment. He tells Cab, "Sex can be riveting. Make you feel like a damn god. But I also know that even when you have as much sex as you can stand in one night, you still feel empty again in the morning" (45). Cab, who is presumably too young to agree with this sentiment, insists that "you just have sex again in the morning," but Randall is not persuaded: "It doesn't matter how much sex you have, it doesn't do for us what we think it will. As fond of it as we are, sex just doesn't work. It will not meet our desperate need for union. It will not release us from our separateness, and it will not put us in genuine contact with another human being" (45). Norman suggests here that men and women expect too much from their romantic relationships and are therefore perpetually disappointed.

But Charlotte is rejecting more than just passion. A decision to turn away from romance in favor of artistic work would make sense, especially for a woman writer, but that is clearly not her intent. On the contrary, Charlotte later reveals to Randall, "I will write no more finely wrought novels, no more essays, no more book reviews, or think pieces. I will scribble no more introductions, blurbs, lists of favorite little known novels. I will teach no more, raise no more money, play no part in public life" (36). What's not entirely clear is what she *will* do. She claims to want to devote herself to the care of a terminally ill aunt named Frances and nicknamed Bunny (who may or may not be an actual aunt, and who may or may not be an actual person).

The audience does, however, learn the fates of all three of the play's other characters. Georgeanne reveals that she and Cab are later married in Savannah, Georgia, while Randall marries Georgeanne's mother. Cab improbably becomes an Atlanta architect, while Georgeanne becomes a French teacher at Norman's alma mater, Agnes Scott College in Atlanta. The couple has two sons. As Georgeanne also reveals, "We never saw Charlotte again but according to her letters, she busied herself taking walks, sleeping and reading, making tea and growing flowers. Randall believes she did none of those things, but who can say" (69). All they know for certain is that she published several volumes of "very direct, very sensual poetry," which leads them to believe that "whatever Charlotte really did for the rest of her life, we can draw no other conclusion than that she was very happy" (69). Although this epilogue reveals that they have come to bury Charlotte, Norman gives her the play's last words, a brief, nine-line poem (or excerpt of a poem).

Norman implies that despite her disavowals, Charlotte *did* want to write and that what she really wanted to renounce were the time-consuming romantic relationships and irksome professional responsibilities—such as reviewing books, writing introductions and blurbs for others' books, teaching, and fundraising—that distracted her from her art. Just as Ginger in *Trudy Blue* needs to develop a certain salutary selfishness in order to experience pleasure in life, so, too, does Charlotte need to renounce the world in order to enjoy it once again.

A ninety-minute play with no intermission, *Last Dance* was originally produced by the Manhattan Theatre Club in New York City. The play opened off Broadway on June 3, 2003, and closed a month later, on July 6. The (exclusively male) reviewers criticized what they saw as the play's thin character development, annoyingly epigrammatic style, and implausible central conceit (see, for example, Ben Brantley, "Earthy Liaisons"; Charles Isherwood, rev. of *Last Dance;* and John Simon, "Southern Comforts"). The most egregiously harsh comment came from Charles Isherwood, who, writing for *Variety,* called the play "staggeringly bad." Lynne Meadow, the artistic director of the Manhattan Theatre Club, had chosen to direct this play herself. She was considerably more charitable in her assessment of *Last Dance:* "Marsha writes about women in such a particular way; she is expressing things that other women haven't expressed" (qtd. in Gener 21).

CHAPTER 9

Writing for a World of Spectators
Television Work

Norman has commented candidly on her choice to balance theater work with writing for television and film because of the more secure financial compensation for the latter. She has also spoken openly (and somewhat disparagingly) about the limitations of screenwriting: "Television has created a world full of spectators. Theatre always creates a world of participants" (Hatcher 188).

"My Shadow"
The Face of a Stranger

The Face of a Stranger, a television movie starring Gena Rowlands and Tyne Daly, first aired on CBS on December 29, 1991, and Rowlands won a Primetime Emmy Award for outstanding actress in a miniseries or special for her role as Pat. Norman told an interviewer that she was "quite proud" of the piece (Beattie 292). Originally given the working title "My Shadow," Norman's script was based on an essay by Mary Stuart first published in the May 16, 1988, issue of *New York* magazine.

The story concerns the slow-growing friendship of a wealthy housewife, Pat, and a homeless bag lady, Dollie Madison. After their accidental encounter, Pat offers Dollie an umbrella she asks for, buys her boots at her request, and eventually takes her to a shoe store, when Dollie rejects the boots for not being sexy enough. Pat's circle of family and friends conspires to keep the two women apart, calling security when Dollie pushes her way into Pat's apartment and telling Pat that if she gives Dollie boots today, Dollie will want a coat from her tomorrow. Pat's daughter, Tina, is incredulous that her mother would waste her time on such a person.

Pat is impatient with those who do not understand her concern for Dollie, telling the doorman that anyone can suddenly experience misfortune. Then Pat's husband, Richard, dies suddenly and unexpectedly, and she learns that she must give up their apartment to pay the debts he leaves behind. Pat attempts to find a job but soon realizes that because she has few marketable skills and no recent work experience, her chances of success are negligible. Norman implies that a woman's social standing is often completely contingent on her husband's health and his financial management skills.

Dollie holds her own in what—because of the difference in their material comforts—might initially seem like an unequal relationship. Pat admires Dollie for being able to wear a hat that Pat had once given to the thrift store because she was unable to carry it off herself. Dollie offers her advice on living alone and reassures her that she will be fine. Dollie even agrees to accompany Pat to the cemetery to visit Richard's grave, a journey that Pat has not been able to bring herself to do on her own.

Dollie recites the nursery rhyme "Little Bo-Peep" and begins calling Pat "Peep." When she drops off a fruitcake at the front door after Richard's death, she tells the doorman it's from Bo Peep. (Interestingly, Pat does not care for fruitcake any more than Dollie cared for the practical boots.) She later recites the nursery rhyme again in the hospital. The rhyme suggests that Dollie, like Little Bo-Peep, has lost something she does not know how to find—and by extension, so has Pat. In Dollie's case, it is her daughter. In Pat's, the implication is that it is herself.

Pat soon begins to move on, going through her husband's clothes to give them away and beginning a relationship with David, a male friend from college. She gradually learns from Dollie how to be herself again, choosing to sleep with David, find an inexpensive apartment, move out of the one she shared with Richard, and wear a dress that is not typical for her—perhaps in response to Dollie's comment that her earlier outfit didn't really suit her. Dollie, on the other hand, deteriorates. She is attacked by young thugs who injure her so severely that she must be rushed to the hospital, and it is days before she gives the hospital authorities Pat's name and contact information.

Dollie turns down Pat's cash, refuses to stay in a shelter, bites a doctor trying to help her, and douses herself with water. When the two women come across a fire burning in a trash can, Dollie responds with hysteria and dissociative behavior so alarming that a passing policeman approaches her to take her in for a psychiatric evaluation, but Dollie eludes him. Tracing the clues from Dollie's mutterings, Pat gradually learns that Dollie's former home burned and was abandoned, and one of the locals blames Dollie for setting the fire, which killed two people, including Dollie's daughter. It is not clear whether Dollie's apparent mental illness is a cause or a result of her poverty and homelessness, although a social worker's comments suggest that the Reagan era's deinstitutionalization of the mentally ill may be the primary cause of Dollie's homelessness.

Consistent with the "greed is good" attitude of the era, Pat's daughter, Tina (played by Cynthia Nixon in the movie), expresses values that seem primarily materialistic. Pat finds it difficult to like Tina's fiancé, Kevin, who announces their impending marriage without bothering to propose to Tina first and is an enthusiastic capitalist. Dollie disrupts Pat's meeting with Kevin's parents to plan the wedding, and Tina blames her mother's weird decision to befriend Dollie when Kevin postpones their wedding. When Tina finally reveals that Kevin has repeatedly cheated on her, she reconciles with her mother, acknowledging her bravery, and in a moment of rare emotional honesty, Pat tells Tina how much she loves her. Tina responds by generously paying for the limousine that takes the two women to the cemetery.

Afterward, Dollie asks to be dropped off at the bus station. Pat tries to insist that she return to the rehab house, but Dollie, characteristically, rejects Pat's attempts to fit her into a conventional lifestyle, preferring instead to make her own choices, however flawed they might be. The film is reminiscent of *Third and Oak* and *A Cooler Climate,* also dramas in which two women bond despite class differences. The working title recalls the psychology of Carl Jung, in which an individual's "shadow" represents the unacknowledged, unconscious dark side to his or her personality. Norman's title thus suggests that Dollie is the darker side of Pat's genteel, ladylike personality: Dollie wears the hat Pat had donated to the thrift store, Dollie wears the outrageous dresses that Pat is afraid to wear, and Dollie survives the bag-lady lifestyle that Pat fears will become her own. Even Dollie's loss of her daughter has echoes in Pat's concern that Tina's marriage will take her away from Pat. Dollie represents the freer, stronger self that Pat longs to be.

Unlikely Friendship

A Cooler Climate (1999)

Based on the 1990 novel of the same name by Zena Collier, *A Cooler Climate* is a made-for-television movie that originally aired on the premium cable channel Showtime on August 22, 1999. Directed by Susan Seidelman, who had directed *Desperately Seeking Susan, A Cooler Climate* focuses on the unlikely friendship between two women in very different economic circumstances. Two-time Oscar winner Sally Field plays Iris Prue, a woman compelled to take a job as a live-in housekeeper after the end of her twenty-six-year marriage. She comes to the picturesque seaside village of Steveston to work for Leo and Paula Tanner, a theatrical attorney and his wife. Through flashbacks to Iris's previous life, Norman reveals that Iris refused the community property and alimony she was entitled to after her divorce because she wanted a fresh start; her imprudent decision explains why Paula discovers a stack of unpaid bills in Iris's room. Iris's daughter, Callie, blames her for the divorce and, in a flashback, refuses to lend her mother money even after Iris is fired from an earlier retail job.

Paula, played by two-time Oscar nominee Judy Davis, initially treats Iris rudely and is an unreasonably demanding employer. But Paula's nineteen-year-old daughter, Beth, soon reveals the flaws in her mother's seemingly perfect life: her friends lie to her, Beth avoids her, and her husband is unfaithful. Beth, who has a history of substance abuse, and her latest boyfriend steal money and jewelry from her mother and abruptly leave the country, and then Leo suddenly leaves Paula after twenty-one years of marriage to pursue his twenty-three-year-old girlfriend. Exasperated by Paula's depressive behavior afterward, Iris convinces her to go for a walk. The two women have an angry confrontation in which Iris confesses that she was miserable for the last ten years of her marriage but never said anything, instead falling into an affair that cost Iris her marriage, her daughter, her home, her furniture, and even her car. Fleeing from Paula, a distraught Iris slips on a steep, rocky hillside and breaks her leg. As a result of this emotional crisis, the two develop a new intimacy: Paula praises Iris afterward for working so hard to rebuild her life and asks her if her relationship with Jack Kelly, the sculptor she has been dating, is serious. As the plot resolves, Paula reconciles with Beth. Iris lands a position as the Steveston Inn's new director of guest relations, and she, too, is reconciled with her daughter.

The movie's hopeful ending differs markedly from the book, which has no fraught confrontation and instead ends with Paula's suicide and its emotional aftermath. Reviews of the movie were lukewarm at best (see, for example, Gates and King), and television critic Howard Rosenberg of the *Los Angeles Times* was particularly critical of the ending, which he perceived as excessively sentimental. Nevertheless, Field and Davis were each nominated for a Primetime Emmy Award for outstanding lead actress in a miniseries or movie, as well as for a Screen Actors Guild Award for outstanding performance by a female actor in a television movie or miniseries. Norman was nominated for a Writers Guild of America Award for her adaptation of the novel into a teleplay.

Doing His Job Better Than He Did

Custody of the Heart

Custody of the Heart, a made-for-television movie based on the novel *A Woman's Place* by Barbara Delinsky, premiered on the Lifetime cable network on August 28, 2000. Norman was both the screenwriter and the co–executive producer of the film, which starred Lorraine Bracco as Claire Raphael, a mother of two who runs her own furniture-design business. Her unemployed husband, a former stockbroker played by Martin Donovan, retaliates for her career success by unexpectedly divorcing her and suing her for full custody of their children. Claire must fight for her children after he charges her with being an unfit mother.

It is clear from the beginning of the movie that the marriage is troubled. Dennis, Claire's husband, offers halfhearted congratulations when he learns she is to receive an award, and he complains when she has the neighbors over for dinner after previously agreeing not to invite guests over on school nights. He is particularly frustrated when she tells him about her latest plans for yet another business trip. When she returns, he has dispatched their two children to his mother's and announces that he is suing Claire for divorce. She is handed a court order to vacate the family home, and when she argues with him, the police arrive to threaten her with arrest if she does not leave immediately.

The next day, a stunned Claire learns from her lawyer that her husband is seeking full custody of the children, child support, alimony, and half of her business. Her attorney tells her that he has been seeing more of this approach from men whose spouses are the family's primary breadwinner, perhaps because men are trying to get even for the way they have historically been treated in divorce cases. Her friend Alice suggests jealousy as Dennis's motive because, Alice suggests, Claire did Dennis's job better than Dennis could.

When Dennis and Claire together tell the children that they plan to divorce, Johnny and Kiki are predictably distraught. Johnny eventually calls a child-abuse hotline, and the police respond by investigating. Dennis tells Claire that the police might take the children away and call them unfit parents, and she snaps that that is exactly what Dennis had done to her. When a police officer gently tells Johnny that the only choice the juvenile judge can make is to remove him from *both* his parents, he reconsiders. Claire learns from a telephone call from her sister that her mother has died, and Dennis relents enough to let her take both children to the funeral. Alone, Dennis runs into Claire's business partner, Brody, in a bar and confesses that he is afraid to try again to reenter the workforce because he has already lost three upper-management positions. He is also troubled because he feels that his family no longer needs him.

Perhaps as a result of this newfound honesty with himself, Dennis stands up to his cutthroat divorce attorney and visits Claire at her new home, a decommissioned lighthouse, where they finally have an honest conversation. He admits he blamed her for her success, and she tells him that her feelings for her business pale in comparison to what she feels for him and the children—although it is difficult to see why she would want to reconcile with a man who had called her an unfit mother and asked a judge to order her to leave her own home. While she tells him she does not want to lose him, he says that he will have to start over and insists that he cannot do so with her because she makes him feel diminished. They meet with a mediator for a much more amicable divorce and agree to share joint custody of the children. The movie ends on an upbeat note with the presentation of Claire's Woman of the Year award. Although the movie is heavy-handed at times, as reviewers noted (Kelleher, "Picks & Pans"; Linan), Norman brings a strong feminist sensibility to this story of reversed gender roles, as, for example, when Claire must face a conservative Catholic judge unsympathetic to working mothers.

The Dangers of Fairy Tales

The Audrey Hepburn Story

Norman wrote the teleplay for *The Audrey Hepburn Story,* a "somewhat sensationalized" made-for-television movie about the life of film actress Audrey Hepburn (Forman and Spencer 2489). The film, which first aired as a three-hour movie on ABC on March 27, 2000, starred Jennifer Love Hewitt in the title role. Reviews were tepid (although it should perhaps be noted that most television reviewers were male—see, for example, Gallo, Pardi, and Tucker), and Love Hewitt was singled out for her presumption in taking on such an ambitious role.

Norman's script opens with Hepburn playing her most iconic movie role, Holly Golightly in *Breakfast at Tiffany's,* the 1961 film based on the novel by Truman Capote. Flashbacks reveal Hepburn's earlier life, beginning with her father's departure when she was eight years old, an event that—according to this script—haunted Hepburn for years. She is still miserable at fourteen, in part because at that age she understands that her ignoble father disseminates Nazi propaganda through the London-based European Press Institute. Norman depicts Hepburn's arrival at boarding school and her early ballet training, as well as her persistent efforts to contact her unresponsive father until a brief reunion before she leaves school because of the impending war. Audrey's performance at the Amsterdam Ballet is melodramatically interrupted by air raid sirens and the announcement that the Germans have invaded Holland. In a curious meta-reference to another of her works, Norman's typescript has Hepburn reading *The Secret Garden* aloud to her grandfather as the city is bombed, although that scene does not appear in the finished movie.

Hepburn joins the Resistance after her uncle is executed by the Nazis in retaliation for the bombing of a German train. She is given dangerous assignments and must act to avoid capture. Norman also dramatizes Hepburn's crushing disappointment when her ballet teacher tells her that she does not have what it takes to become a professional ballerina. The screenplay chronicles her debut as a chorus girl in the West End production of *High Button Shoes,* an early relationship with Marcel Le Bon, her film debut in a one-line role, a serious romance with James Hanson, and her triumphant Broadway debut in Colette's *Gigi*. Unable to reconcile the demands of work with her romantic life, Hepburn ends the relationship with Hanson as she begins work on the film *Roman Holiday.* But she falls in love with William Holden, one of her two costars on *Sabrina,* and is eager to marry him until she abruptly breaks off the relationship when she learns that, because of a vasectomy, he cannot give her children. She instead marries actor Mel Ferrer, whom Norman shows controlling Hepburn's career and taking credit for her successes.

Norman foreshadows Hepburn's eventual commitment to the work of UNICEF through her joy at joining Sister Luc in her charitable work assisting orphans in Africa in preparation for the film *The Nun's Story.* In a later scene in Norman's typescript (but not the finished movie), Hepburn clarifies that she wants to give back because she herself has repeatedly been saved by others, including her mother, the Allied soldiers that liberated Holland, and her friends.

The screenplay contains repeated fairy-tale motifs. Music from *Sleeping Beauty* plays when Hepburn spends time with her father, according to stage directions in the typescript. In the typescript, but again, not in the finished movie, she experiences a hallucination of her father while she hides in a cellar to avoid capture by the Nazis, and her father compares one of her childhood dresses to Cinderella's (43). In both the screenplay and the movie, Audrey's friend Kay compares James Hanson to Prince Charming, and his home on the Yorkshire moors resembles a castle. Norman suggests through these motifs that fairy tales are dangerously seductive for women but ultimately untrustworthy and unfulfilling. Joseph, Audrey's father, is finally indifferent to her, not the warm, half-imagined father of her early childhood, and she ultimately rejects James because otherwise she would not be able to devote enough time to the career she so enjoys.

Food is a locus of control for Hepburn throughout Norman's screenplay. She struggles to eat pastries for the *Breakfast at Tiffany's* scene because the pastries remind her too vividly of her father's departure. She later collapses from hunger after her ordeal in the cellar (45). She is enchanted by the chocolate bars handed out by the American liberators and later ensures that the *Breakfast at Tiffany's* crew has chocolate available because she enjoyed it so much after the war. In the screenplay, but not the finished movie, she faints from hunger while dancing (33), and still her ballet teacher orders her to lose weight (52). In other scenes not in the film, she orders sandwiches, cookies, and cake once she learns the prospect of a career in ballet is over but is so distraught she is unable to eat anything when the food arrives (58); she pushes her plate away, again unable to eat, when her husband schedules her for too many movies and too much time apart when all she wants is to become a mother. Norman has Audrey later describe an overly rigid diet in which she eats the same food every day (147). She also rejects food when she is disappointed in her final meeting with her father. Hepburn repeatedly refuses food to signal disagreement or unhappiness.

Like most of Norman's female protagonists, Hepburn has a fraught relationship with her mother, Baroness Ella van Heemstra. Given Audrey's difficulties with food, it is not a coincidence that her mother works for a time in a restaurant (53). It is clear that Ella loves her daughter; she traded cigarettes obtained from the soldiers to get the penicillin Audrey needed to recover her health. But Ella also repeatedly destroyed letters from Audrey's father because, she says, she did not want him to hurt Audrey any more. In an apparently intentional ambiguity, it is not clear whether Hepburn's miscarriage arises as a delayed result of a riding accident on set or as a violent reaction to her discovery that her mother has withheld her father's letters from her. Mother and daughter are finally reconciled when, after a final rejection by her father, Audrey recognizes that her mother's solicitude was justified.

Progress in America

Samantha: An American Girl Holiday

Norman returned to her theme of female friendship across class lines in *Samantha: An American Girl Holiday,* a 2004 made-for-television movie for children. The eighty-six-minute movie first aired on the WB Network on November 23, 2004. The script Norman wrote, which was later published in a keepsake book featuring twenty-five color stills from the movie, was based on a series of six novels by Valerie Tripp, Susan S. Adler, and Maxine Rose Schur. All six centered around Samantha Parkington, an orphaned girl growing up in her grandmother's home in Mount Bedford, New York, in 1904. American Girl, a Wisconsin-based subsidiary of Mattel, manufactured an eighteen-inch "Samantha" doll that the books and movie were designed to cross-promote.

In the movie, nine-year-old Samantha, played by AnnaSophia Robb, befriends Nellie O'Malley, the neighbors' young maid, and since Nellie's mother has recently died, the two girls bond through their shared experience of parental loss. Through their friendship Samantha learns about the hardships faced by a child who works first in a factory and then as a maid. Samantha teaches Nellie to read even though her grandmother, whom she calls "Grandmary," would disapprove. Grandmary, played by Mia Farrow, insists upon class difference: "The secret to a happy household is for everyone to know their place" (Norman, *Samantha* 24).

Samantha's Uncle Gard, played by Jordan Bridges, arrives with the surprising news that he plans to marry Cornelia Pitt. Played by Rebecca Mader, Cornelia is a staunchly feminist young woman who supports women's suffrage. Although Samantha misses the days when she had Uncle Gard's undivided attention, she agrees to Cornelia's request that she be Cornelia's bridesmaid. When the bridal veil accidentally catches fire and is ruined, Samantha conquers her jealousy and graciously offers Cornelia her late mother's veil.

Samantha travels to New York City to stay with Uncle Gard and Aunt Cornelia, and she and Nellie exchange letters for a time. When Nellie falls silent, Samantha discovers that Nellie's father has died, and Nellie and her two younger sisters have been placed in a New York City orphanage that allows only relatives to visit. Cornelia calls on a wealthy and influential friend involved in the suffrage movement to prevail upon the matron to allow them to visit, and they are dismayed by the conditions within the orphanage. Samantha returns on her own later and helps the three girls escape to live secretly in the attic of the home where Samantha is staying. When one of the girls, Bridget, becomes ill, Samantha visits Nellie at the factory where she works and is amazed at the cold, the unsanitary conditions, and the ruthlessness of the management. She ultimately confesses to her aunt and uncle in order to get medical attention for Bridget.

Samantha reveals how much she has learned when she delivers her speech on progress in America: "Children are hurt in these places. I know[.] I saw one. If our factories can hurt children, then we have not made good progress in America" (127). Because the speech she gives does not match the much less critical speech she submitted earlier in writing, her teacher disqualifies Samantha's effort. The teleplay ends with a series of happy endings: a marriage to a longtime admirer for Grandmary, generous holiday donations for the orphanage, and—most implausibly—a permanent home with Uncle Gard and Aunt Cornelia, not just for Samantha but for all three of her friends as well.

Reviewers made much of the movie as a marketing device for American Girl dolls and criticized what they saw as its excessive sentimentality (Kelleher, rev. of *Samantha;* Stanley, "Doll"). While admittedly sentimental, however, the movie is not falsely nostalgic, highlighting instead the terrifying vulnerability of poor children in Progressive Era America.

"Albatross" and "Brother's Keeper"
Law & Order: Criminal Intent (2007)

Norman wrote the teleplays for two episodes of the hour-long police procedural drama *Law & Order: Criminal Intent,* which aired on NBC for six seasons before moving to the USA cable network for its final four seasons. The second spinoff (after *Law & Order: Special Victims Unit*) from the original *Law & Order* television series, *Criminal Intent* focuses on the criminal's motives, and episodes usually end with a confession (rather than the courtroom trial more typical of episodes of the original *Law & Order* series). Set in New York City, the crime drama focuses on the NYPD's Major Case Squad, which specifically investigates high-profile cases.

Norman has spoken openly about what a pleasurable experience her work for the series was: "I enjoyed the camaraderie of it, the tech stuff, the men, the food, that's all fun . . . I like the pay. And Warren [Leight, a writer and executive producer of the series] created a staff that was all playwrights—so that was fun, too, seeing Gina Gionfriddo and Jackie Reingold and Diana Son every day" (Garrison 40).

The two episodes for which Norman wrote the teleplays are "Albatross," which first aired February 6, 2007, and "Brother's Keeper," which aired February 20, 2007, both in the show's sixth season. (Both episodes are currently available on DVD and on the streaming service Amazon Prime.) In "Albatross," two men perform a historical enactment of the 1804 duel between Alexander Hamilton and Aaron Burr. One of the men, a prominent judge, dies as a result of a gunshot wound that police quickly realize is not a result of the duel but the work of a sniper. Because the two men changed clothes at the last minute, detectives realize that the other man, George Pagolis, was probably the intended target, and suspicion falls on his wife, Maureen Pagolis, a popular politician known for her support of feminist causes. She has ample motive: her husband is a womanizer, his mob connections and criminal actions have repeatedly jeopardized her political career, and one scene strongly implies that he is abusive to the point of marital rape. When the sniper, a hired killer, also turns up dead, the Major Case Squad works to resolve the case.

The episode features unusual cuts to what journalists have traditionally called "man-on-the-street interviews," in which members of the general public comment on the news—in this case, the politician and her troubled marriage. Maureen's constituents do not understand why she stays married, given her husband's shameless philandering, and some express doubts about how she can possibly remain innocent when he is so obviously corrupt. Norman explains Maureen's decision to stay in the marriage as concern for their sons and how they would react to a divorce. As for the public's second concern, she is clearly no longer innocent; George has successfully corrupted her with his persistent physical and psychological violence, as the ending makes evident. More broadly, however, these man-on-the street interviews demonstrate vividly how Maureen's life is subjected to the attention and critique of the general public, who feel entitled to judge her choices and evaluate her character and the quality of her marriage without even knowing her. Norman is commenting here on the ways in which politicians and other celebrities—perhaps especially those who are female—are scrutinized and publicly criticized.

The title "Albatross" is an allusion to Samuel Taylor Coleridge's 1798 poem "The Rime of the Ancient Mariner," in which a mariner encounters a man on his way to a wedding and tells a haunting story. He had once long ago killed an albatross—a kind of sea bird—that had just led the ship on which he was a sailor out of an ice jam. After he shoots the albatross with his cross-bow, the ship becomes stuck once more, this time because there is no wind, and the crew, nearly mad with thirst, forces the mariner to wear the dead albatross around his neck as a punishment for bringing them such cursed luck. The ship encounters a haunted ship on which a skeleton named Death and a ghostly woman named Night-mare Life-in-Death play dice for the souls of the crew. One by one all of his shipmates die, leaving the mariner the only one alive. To expiate his sin, the rescued mariner must wander the earth, telling his terrible story to those he encounters. Norman's use of the title "Albatross" for this episode suggests that perhaps Maureen's husband is her albatross, and when she happened to learn beforehand of the plan to kill him, she failed to intervene, thus bringing a haunting curse upon herself and her family.

In "Brother's Keeper," a fundamentalist minister, the Reverend Calvin Riggins, and a skeptical scientist, Dr. James Corliss, engage in a public debate as part of a ten-city tour pitting faith against science. Their New York appearance suddenly becomes a melee when the scientist angrily accuses God of vindictiveness. Marjorie, the preacher's wife (and a friend of Corliss's), is rushed out of the ensuing near-riot for her own safety but is found dead on the stairs soon afterward. Although her death is initially attributed to an accident caused by her labyrinthitis (an illness characterized by extreme vertigo), an autopsy reveals that she had been shaken to death. Just before her death, she was given a DVD left for her by Diego, a rent-boy whom her husband had paid for gay sex. Diego resents the minister's preaching about the sinfulness of homosexuality and wants to blackmail him into silence on the issue of gay marriage. Corliss claims that Cal had aspired to be the next Billy Graham. When Detective Bobby Goren confronts Cal about his sexual misconduct, Cal confesses that he knew what he was doing was wrong but was unable to stop himself.

Financial records lead Detective Alexandra Eames to discover that Corliss has a seventeen-year-old mentally disabled son, Jimmy, whose care he supports financially. He writes "Cleaning services" on the memo line of the checks he writes Alminia Perez for Jimmy's care: She cleans Jimmy right out of Corliss's life. Although Corliss cannot bring himself to visit Jimmy, he admits that when the minister referred to the inability of an unnamed, "very intelligent man" to raise his intellectually disabled teenage son, Corliss became furious that Marjorie had told Cal his secret—so furious that he half-inadvertently killed her.

Norman's invented tale of a hidden son with mental retardation sounds suspiciously similar to what journalist Suzanna Andrews revealed in *Vanity Fair* magazine about American playwright Arthur Miller six months after the show aired: he had had a child named Daniel with Down syndrome whom Miller institutionalized and excised from his life (except for a reported bequest in his will). Miller did not mention Daniel in his memoir, *Timebends,* and rarely visited his son, even though his wife visited Daniel weekly (Andrews). Perhaps Norman had heard rumors about the story (not impossible, given the story's relevance to the theater world), or perhaps her imaginings just coincidentally and eerily anticipated the real-life revelations. Certainly it was not unusual in mid-twentieth-century America to institutionalize a mentally retarded child, and Miller was not the only parent to respond to the stigmatizing experience with silence and psychological denial.

Norman is interested here, as in her play *Traveler in the Dark,* about the conflict between faith and science in American culture. She suggests in this dark teleplay that faith is almost inevitably hypocritical but that science puts too much faith in intelligence, sometimes at the cost of human compassion and connection. Both faith and science, she suggests, are equally ready to betray women. Marjorie tries to reconcile these two opposites, telling her husband about Corliss's secret in order to evoke his compassion, but Cal instead uses the information to taunt Corliss, who, angry over her perceived betrayal, shakes her to death in an attempt to discover why she had revealed his secret to her husband.

An important subplot also contributes to the story. Detective Bobby Goren's mentally ill mother, played by Broadway and movie star Rita Moreno, is dying and repeatedly asks about her other son, Frank, who is clearly her favorite. Perhaps as a result of the schizophrenia for which she has been institutionalized, she illogically insists that if Frank were here, she would not have gone through the rigors of chemotherapy because Frank would have taken care of her. Bobby coincidentally runs into Frank later on the street, so financially destitute that he waits in line at a church's soup kitchen. Although Frank says the church helped him get clean, he is red-eyed, sniffing, and almost furtive in his behavior, suggesting ongoing substance abuse. Bobby sympathetically offers his estranged brother cash, literally gives him the coat off his back, and plans to take him to visit their mother on Sunday. Bobby also tucks one of his business cards into Frank's pocket in case Frank ever needs his help.

In a later scene with Bobby and his mother, the audience is left to surmise that Frank never showed, but Bobby protects him by telling their mother that

Frank is fine and that he has seen him recently coming out of church. In the episode's somber final scene, the medical examiner has called Bobby because a corpse she is examining has the detective's card in his pocket. Bobby views the body, but it is not his brother. He says defensively that his brother must have sold the coat because, after all, everyone needs more money.

The teleplay's title refers to the biblical story of the first murder (Genesis 4:1–15). Cain murders his brother, Abel, out of jealousy, and when the Lord afterwards asks him where his brother is, Cain replies disingenuously that he does not know: "Am I my brother's keeper?" (Genesis 4:10). The implication is that, contrary to Cain's assumption, the answer is yes. Each of the three men in the *Criminal Intent* episode fails to "keep" his brother: Instead of showing Corliss compassion, Cal uses Corliss's secret against him in a public debate. Corliss rejects his disabled son, perhaps because he overvalues intelligence; more seriously, he murders his friend Marjorie. And while Bobby does *try* to take care of Frank, to be his brother's keeper, Frank carelessly sells his brother's gift of a coat (presumably for drug money) and does not even bother to take the business card his brother gave him out of the coat's pocket.

Interestingly, all three of the men Bobby encounters are gripped by irrational and ultimately self-destructive compulsions they find themselves unable to control: Cal's attraction to a gay male escort and their recreational drug use, Corliss's violent rage over what he perceives as Marjorie's betrayal of his secret to Cal, and Frank's addiction. When Corliss calls the reverend's congregation a group of fanatics invested in irrationality, Bobby points out that murder is often irrational. Norman suggests in this teleplay that neither faith nor science fully accounts for irrationality in human beings.

The Talking Cure

In Treatment (2009)

Based closely on the successful Israeli television series *Be'Tipul, In Treatment* is an HBO drama about middle-aged psychoanalyst Paul Weston, played by Gabriel Byrne. The first season included forty-three half-hour episodes, each airing on a different night of the work week; the second season included thirty-five episodes, of which Norman wrote seven, all for the "Gina" episodes in which Paul met with his own psychotherapist and clinical supervisor, Gina, played by Dianne Wiest. The second season's executive producer was Warren Leight, a Tony Award-winning playwright who had previously worked on *Law & Order: Criminal Intent;* it was very likely Leight who recruited Norman to work on both series. As noted previously, he was known for hiring established playwrights to work on television scripts for the series he ran. Other playwrights writing teleplays for *In Treatment* included Keith Bunin, Sarah Treem, and Jacquelyn Reingold. It is easy to see why the show's structure—"essentially a chain of two-person, one-act plays without action, sets, or pop-music cues" (Stanley)—would have attracted the interest of serious playwrights.

During the first four episodes each week, Paul Weston responds to each of his troubled patients calmly and thoughtfully, even when they behave seductively, curse at him, break down, or otherwise "act out." His clients include men and women and range in age from an elementary school student to a corporate executive approaching retirement age. Because of his gravity and imperturbability, Paul seems like the sane center of a profoundly troubled world. Only in the final episode each week, authored by Norman, does the audience learn that Paul has his own troubles coping with past traumatic experiences, including his mother's suicide many years earlier, his complicated relationship with his father, his divorce, and his professional difficulties, including a malpractice lawsuit. Paul behaves in the same contradictory, self-defeating ways as his patients do, resisting Gina's advice and irrationally hiding his concerns from her until she probes for details.

It might initially seem that Norman deliberately punctures the stereotype of the therapist as all knowing and wise, instead presenting the doctor as needing as much help as his patients. But in the final episode each week, Norman perpetuates the stereotype, simply transferring the wisdom and omniscience from Paul to Gina. Gina repeatedly insists on the necessary limits to what the therapist can do and emphasizes the need for boundaries and detachment for the protection of both the therapist and the patient. Her insistence that only the patient can change his or her own life confirms that individual autonomy remains a central tenet of Norman's work.

CHAPTER 10

Later Musicals

The Red Shoes, The Color Purple, The Trumpet of the Swan, The Master Butcher's Singing Club, and *The Bridges of Madison County*

The Red Shoes

Jule Styne, the eighty-seven-year-old composer of a host of successful musicals, including *Gypsy, Peter Pan, Funny Girl,* and *Gentlemen Prefer Blondes,* first proposed the idea of a Broadway musical based on *The Red Shoes,* the 1948 film of the same name. A classic melodrama, the film chronicles a ballerina's irreconcilable conflict between her dance impresario and the man she loves, a conflict that ends only with her suicide. Styne had written the score for the film, which starred Moira Shearer. The film was very loosely based, in turn, on a disturbing fairy tale by Danish author Hans Christian Andersen in which a young motherless girl who insists on wearing red shoes to church feels compelled to dance obsessively until she finally begs an executioner to cut off her feet. Even then, she is prevented from returning to church by the dancing shoes until she humbles herself enough to repent of her sin and beg for God's help. The Broadway musical was instead set in a Russian ballet troupe in 1920s Europe. The musical's centerpiece ballet is based on the Anderson story, a cautionary tale about the dangers of women's vanity.

Producer Martin Starger hired Norman in 1991; she became the third writer to work on the book. Director Susan Schulman signed on a few months later; Schulman and Norman had previously worked together on *The Secret Garden.* Starger fired Schulman after a couple of workshops received mixed reviews and before Broadway rehearsals began. Actor Roger Rees, the musical's leading man, was also abruptly fired and replaced by Steve Barton, his understudy.

Hollywood director Stanley Donen was then recruited to direct, although he had never before directed on Broadway. Films he had directed included *Singin' in the Rain, On the Town,* and *Funny Face.* Bob Merrill, who had worked with Styne on *Funny Girl,* was brought in to help Norman with the lyrics and received a credit under the name Paul Stryker (Richards, rev. of *The Red Shoes*), and Norman has said that only one song she wrote remained in the final version of the musical (Pringle).

The musical went through an unusual fifty-one previews before opening on Broadway. Although some reviewers praised the dancing of lead actress Margaret Illmann and the choreography of Lar Lubovitch, the reviews were largely negative (see, for example, Gerard, Judith Green, Goldner, Johnson, Richards, Shapiro and Peyser, and Winship). Sadly, it closed after only five performances, losing almost $8 million. The producer was later criticized because the show was closed before it could run long enough to qualify for Tony nominations (Weber).

Styne and Donen publicly blamed Norman for the show's failure, while Norman countered by blaming the producer and Donen (Weber; Mootz, "Marsha"). Press reports suggested that there were conflicting visions of how closely the musical should follow the film and that Norman and the original director, Susan Schulman, among others, felt that following the film too closely would result in a dated show. In particular, they wanted to revise the ending. Norman proposed an ending in which the protagonist, Vicki, does not commit suicide but instead dies onstage when, distracted by a fight between the two men who battle over her, she fails to perform a dangerous stunt successfully (Shapiro and Peyser). Heidi Landesman, set designer for *The Red Shoes* (as well as for *The Secret Garden*) has suggested that the generation gap between Schulman, Norman, choreographer Lar Lubovitch, and herself, who at the time were all between forty and fifty years old, and Starger, sixty-one, Styne, eighty-seven, and Donen, sixty-nine, contributed to the friction (McKerrow). It is also possible that gender differences complicated the situation. Landesman has suggested that the men were more interested in the aging impresario than they were in the ballerina, an attitude the women did not share (McKerrow, Pringle). Fired director Schulman, too, blamed chauvinism for the show's failure (Weber). Norman later indicated that the chief frustration of her disappointing experience with *The Red Shoes* was her lack of control over her own work (Mootz, "Marsha").

The Color Purple

Alice Walker won the Pulitzer Prize for fiction for her 1982 novel *The Color Purple* in 1983, the same year that Norman won the Pulitzer Prize for drama for *'night, Mother.* Therefore, Norman felt a certain connection to the novel and was thrilled when Steven Spielberg invited her to talk to him about the possibility of writing a script for a film of the novel that he planned to produce and direct. She was disappointed to discover, however, that Spielberg felt she was the wrong choice because he could not get past the idea that Jessie in *'night, Mother* had so grievously hurt her mother. He ultimately hired Menno Meyjes, a white man from the Netherlands, to write the screenplay.

"Five or six years ago, when I heard they were working on the musical, I put my hand in the air again and I said, 'Oh, me, me, pick me.' They got back in touch with my agent and me and said, 'No, no, we can't have you; we need a black writer.' And I said, 'Well, of course you do.' And I wished them luck and that was it," Norman has said (Funderburg 21). So Norman was particularly excited to be invited in February 2005 to join the creative team of the Broadway musical, even at that late date: "I've been trying to say yes to *The Color Purple* since 1983" (Funderburg 21). The composer and lyricists had worked on *The Color Purple* for about four years and created approximately twenty songs before Norman became involved with the musical: "I'd been trying to get a chance to work on this project ever since Alice [Walker] and I won the Pulitzer on the same day. I had tried to get to do the movie and they didn't want me. . . . So by the time they asked me, I was really ready" (Garrison 42).

Interestingly, it was Scott Sanders, the show's lead producer and a white man who grew up in St. Petersburg, Florida, who first conceived of the novel as possible source material for a musical. By that time *The Color Purple* already had a distinguished history. In addition to the Pulitzer Prize, Walker's epistolary novel also won the National Book Award, making Walker the first African American woman to win both of those honors. The novel spent weeks on the bestseller list. Spielberg's 1985 film *The Color Purple* starred Whoopi Goldberg, Oprah Winfrey, and Danny Glover and received eleven Academy Award nominations. (It did not win, and ironically, the film that swept the awards that year, receiving eleven nominations and winning seven Oscars, was *Out of Africa,* about the continent's white European colonizers.) A commercial success, *The Color Purple* cost an estimated $15 million to make and grossed more than $98 million in the United States alone, according to the Internet Movie Database.

Chiefly because of the way it portrayed African American men, Spielberg's film of *The Color Purple* was the subject of vigorous controversy. In her memoir about the experience of having the novel filmed, Walker catalogs some of the charges against her work (22) and reprints some of the attacks, including both published articles and personal letters. The Coalition Against Black Exploitation picketed the film at both a benefit showing for the Black Women's Forum in Los Angeles and the Academy Awards (285).

As Rudolph P. Byrd, a professor of American Studies at Emory University, commented in the published memory book of the musical, "No writer in the twentieth century was attacked in the sustained and virulent way that Alice was around this novel. No writer. None. The critique was that Alice Walker and her novel were committed only to an unfair representation of the lives of black men. . . . Spielberg's film was the gasoline that spread the fire" (Funderburg 25). Perhaps in response to that criticism, Norman insisted, "We wanted to return to the book in its treatment of the men. We wanted to give Mister his full journey, which is all the way through to his redemption, to where he understands" (32).

The novel's central character is a downtrodden fourteen-year-old girl named Celie, who was sexually abused by Pa, the man she believes to be her father, and then handed over in marriage to Mister, an abusive man who was in love with her sister. Barely literate, Celie is so isolated in her rural southern poverty that she writes letters to God because no one else is interested enough in her feelings to read them. She mourns the two children she bore, whom Pa has spirited away, and Nettie, the sister from whom she has become separated.

Like many of Norman's protagonists, Celie is a trapped girl struggling to escape from a dangerous family, and she is ultimately triumphant. As Walker says, in a sentence that sounds oddly like something Norman might say, "I like people who refuse to be victims and delight in showing everybody else how this is done" (48). The novel's other women also experience hardships: Sofia, who is married to Mister's son, Harpo, is jailed when she refuses to become the maid of the mayor's wife. She is released into the mayor's custody and compelled to become their maid after all. Squeak, given her nickname because of her high-pitched voice, becomes Harpo's consort in Sofia's absence, and only later do we learn that she has always wanted to become a singer.

Shug Avery, a sexually liberated blues singer, arrives in town, and a dazzled Celie falls in love with her. Shug discovers that Nettie has been writing letters that Mister has intercepted and hidden from Celie. She turns those letters over to a joyous Celie, who learns from the letters that her two children have been living with Nettie, a missionary in Africa. Celie makes a pair of pants for Shug and gradually launches her own business. The novel concludes with the joyous reunion of Celie with her children and Nettie.

In a letter to Danny Glover, Walker acknowledged that the story is based on the lives of her grandparents in the small town of Eatonton, Georgia, where Walker herself grew up as a sharecropper's daughter (Walker 211–13). Despite their obvious differences (racially and sexually), Walker and Norman had a great deal in common. Walker, like Norman, had experienced the same sense of being trapped in a family where she did not belong: "I've often felt that to my family, I have sometimes been a curious, even miraculous, stranger" (171). Just as Norman had had an imaginary friend named Bettering (Forman and Spencer 2490), Alice's sister remembered her speaking to imaginary people as a child (Walker 200).

The song lyrics and an abridged version of Marsha Norman's libretto for the musical were published in *The Color Purple: A Memory Book of the Broadway Musical,* a lavish coffee-table book with a list price of forty dollars. Designed to resemble a family scrapbook, the memory book also includes a foreword by Oprah Winfrey, many color photographs of the musical, interviews with the members of the creative team (including Norman), discussions of costume design and set design for the show, and a chapter on the work's impact.

Part of what attracted Norman to the project was the novel's southern setting and material, which she felt she knew well from her own Kentucky upbringing. As Norman says, "The big thing about the South, which I knew from growing up there, is everybody knows who you are and what you're doing and what you're up against and how you're faring. And because it's a world that's lived outside and in a sense of familiarity, you're constantly being watched" (Funderburg 22). The three gossipy Church Ladies who sing "Mysterious Ways" in the first act function as a Greek chorus, commenting on the characters and action of the play (43).

Norman has said, "One of the hardest things that we had to struggle with was how to incorporate Celie into the Africa story" (30). Norman solved this difficulty by linking the Church Ladies who critically scrutinize Celie with the African women who disapprove of Nettie for teaching girls to read: "And suddenly the audience says, Oh, these women are everywhere" (30). Norman has also said that "the great breakthrough in Africa was equating Africa with Sofia. When you say, Okay, Africa is Sofia, then you really can get that here's this great big powerful force that's also vulnerable to great harm" (30).

Certainly the novel contained difficult material. Producer Roy Furman has said that the novel's themes, including sexual abuse, domestic violence, lesbianism, and the separation of children from their parents (not to mention racism in colonial Africa), made it difficult to persuade potential investors to support the project. He typically responded by pointing out that perhaps they would prefer to invest in a musical about Jews in Czarist Russia facing a pogrom and eventual forced exile—precisely the premise of the hugely successful *Fiddler on the Roof* (27). In other words, he explained, a brilliant creative team can make any theme work for audiences.

Sanders has said, "Some of the criticism we've gotten was that we have too much material in the show, it's too much for people to digest, and it moves too quickly" (31). The musical lasts two hours and forty minutes, and Sanders concedes that some critics would have preferred a more narrowly focused plot: "We are dealing with much more complicated storytelling in *The Color Purple* than a lot of musicals" (31).

Some of *The Color Purple* was entirely "musicalized" (drama conducted entirely in song, as in *Les Miserables*) when Norman arrived and had to be rewritten. For example, Norman felt it was necessary to emphasize in the song "Shug Avery Comin' to Town" how differently men and women responded to Shug's arrival (24)—a theme already present in the novel. As Norman herself put it, "So part of what I did with those songs that already existed was to try to figure out how they became part of the show, instead of isolated performance moments" (24).

Norman felt that in Walker's novel, Celie was an observer rather than a truly active central character: "She's the recording secretary. She writes it all down" (30). Although Celie does have experiences in the novel, other characters are much more interesting, and Sofia and Shug in particular are more attention-getting. As she had done with Mary Lennox in *The Secret Garden,* Norman made Celie much more central in the musical: "In the beginning, what we see is the girls [Celie and her sister, Nettie] in the tree, and they're completely by themselves. And we know from various things that happen during the story that Celie does identify with birds—she sings in that first song that she wants to raise birds. By the end, what you see is that Celie has basically become the tree. And everybody has come back to roost in the branches of Celie. The whole family has, as if they've taken refuge and shelter in her. She has become the family tree" (Funderburg 22).

Norman has confessed to worrying every night that the audience would get up and walk out when Celie and Shug kiss—a development that never occurred (Garrison 38). Norman loved the way in which the audience entered into Celie's journey. In words that could just as easily describe Norman herself, she described Celie as "the girl with no chance, who finally makes it, who finds people to stand with her and makes it through. And helps them too in the process" (Garrison 58). As Norman explained of the musical's conclusion, "This is an awakening. Celie wakes up to what we have all known since moment one of the show. We have all loved her since the beginning. And now she comes to love her" (Funderburg 30).

Although the play that premiered in Georgia opened with a funeral scene, the Broadway version was less somber, opening instead with a scene of Celie and Nettie singing "Huckleberry Pie" and playing a handclap game—invented by Steven Spielberg and Dutch screenwriter Menno Meyjes for the film (Brode 156)—in a tree. Although the next song, "Mysterious Ways," delineates the religious background from which Celie's submissive resignation springs, Norman did not want to show Celie wallowing in self-pity over her admittedly miserable experiences. Norman has said that on opening night, "I felt proud and free and invisible. I felt like I had done a thing that I had wanted to do, which was to convey this story on to the Broadway stage with a sense of joy. That's what I wanted. I wanted to make sure that the triumph of this story made it onto the stage" (Funderburg 183).

Walker said, "What I like most about Marsha's work is that she was very respectful of what was already there and had a real sense of the modernity" (30). Songwriter Allee Willis also praised Norman's willingness to collaborate: "If you say, give me some idea of what you're thinking, most people give a five-word synopsis. Marsha starts spouting out anything that comes to mind. I furiously wrote down whatever she said because I trusted her instincts. Here, she said, 'No one in this town respects me, my father treated me like shit, my woman's sleeping with my wife . . .' We put in order what Marsha was saying and turned it into a lyric" (57). Songwriter Brenda Russell recalled Marsha consoling her when she was crying hysterically over cuts to the work she had done (45).

The Color Purple premiered at the Alliance Theatre in Atlanta, Georgia, in September 2004 for a five-week run. The musical debuted on Broadway on December 1, 2005, and ran for 910 performances before it closed on February 24, 2008, grossing more than $103 million. It received eleven Tony nominations, including for best musical and best book of a musical for Norman.

Kathryn Edney has charged that "*The Color Purple* was rhetorically 'normalized' to align it within the genre conventions of the idealized Broadway musical epitomized by the works of Rodgers and Hammerstein" (227). She pointed out that while many of the show's songs evolved from African American musical traditions, the composers created generic pop songs for Celie in an effort to make her more accessible to white audiences: "By giving her the most 'universal' music to sing as a means of transforming her into a more relatable character, the creators of *The Color Purple* drained Walker's heroine of what makes her such a compelling character in the first place: her unique voice" (244). But the film is vulnerable to similar charges: Walker has publicly criticized what one critic has described as the film's "bland orchestral score" (Morris 124), complaining that it "sounded like it belonged in *Oklahoma*" (Walker 21).

American Idol winner Fantasia Barrino was eventually cast in the lead role of Celie, which helped boost ticket sales. Norman has staunchly defended the director's unconventional casting decision: "Fantasia was *exactly* this girl eight years ago—she was fourteen and pregnant, she was poor and didn't know anybody" (Garrison 38).

Oprah Winfrey produced a revival of *The Color Purple,* which opened on December 10, 2015, in the Bernard B. Jacobs Theatre on Broadway. Cynthia Erivo, who starred in the London production at the Menier Chocolate Factory, played Celie in the revival. Oscar-, Golden Globe– and Grammy-winning performer Jennifer Hudson made her Broadway debut as Shug Avery. The show won the 2016 Tony Award for Best Revival of a Musical. Press reports indicate that Oprah Winfrey, Steven Spielberg, Scott Sanders, and Quincy Jones plan to adapt the musical into a film ("Harpo").

The Trumpet of the Swan: A Novel-Symphony for Actors and Orchestra

Norman worked with composer Jason Robert Brown to adapt *The Trumpet of the Swan: A Novel Symphony for Actors and Orchestra* from E. B. White's 1970 children's novel, *The Trumpet of the Swan.* In the novel, a swan named Louis is born without a voice and instead learns to play a brass trumpet. The "novel symphony," created for a symphony orchestra, actors, and a trumpet soloist, was originally produced as a Kennedy Center commission in December 2008, starring Kathy Bates, Zayd Dohrn, Edward Gero, Lauren Kennedy, Peggity Price, Richard Thomas, Christopher Venditti, and Fred Willard.

John Lithgow, Kathy Bates, Jesse Tyler Ferguson, Martin Short, James Naughton, and Mandy Moore starred in the 2011 production of the "novel symphony" at the Kennedy Center with the National Symphony Orchestra. The 2011 performance was recorded and released on CD and digitally.

The Master Butcher's Singing Club

When Norman adapted Louise Erdrich's novel about German immigrants in her hometown of Argus, North Dakota, for musical theater, Norman pronounced the novel "a big, epic, American tale": "It's this wonderful novel about this moment in North Dakota where a survivor from the Massacre at Wounded Knee can serve as our narrator for a story about the immigrant culture as it begins to move past New York" (Norman and Margulies 26). The project had unusual challenges. For example, Norman has said that Louise Erdrich and the Native actors insisted that the play could not include a reenactment of Wounded Knee because it is considered sacred. She also had to choose her language carefully to reflect historical accuracy: "What I'm saying is, when you are writing outside your own experience, you have to make a real commitment to the truth of the experience, as seen by the people who do live it" (27).

The Master Butchers Singing Club opened at the Guthrie Theatre in Minneapolis, Minnesota, on September 11, 2010, for a scheduled eight-week run. It closed a week earlier than planned because of poor ticket sales.

The Bridges of Madison County

First staged in 2013, *The Bridges of Madison County* is a musical based on the 1992 surprise bestseller by Robert James Waller. The novel had already been made into a 1995 film starring Clint Eastwood and Meryl Streep, who was nominated for an Academy Award for best actress. According to Norman, Waller expressed interest in seeing his novel adapted into a musical, so Aaron Priest, his literary agent, approached playwright and director James Lapine, then best known for *Falsettos, Into the Woods,* and *Sunday in the Park with George,* about the proposed musical, and Lapine referred Priest to Norman (Hetrick, "Brief Encounter"). Norman, who had read the novel years earlier, reread it and then got in touch with Jason Robert Brown, a Tony Award winner for his score for the 1999 musical *Parade,* to ask about the possibility of collaborating on the project. She and Brown, who became the musical's composer and lyricist, had worked together previously on *The Trumpet of the Swan,* a commission from the Kennedy Center, and he had scored her play *Last Dance* at the Manhattan Theatre Club (Evans 44). He had never read the book or seen the movie but had been looking for a new musical, preferably a romantic, operatic project after working on a series of comedies (Evans 44). He told Norman he was looking for his *La Traviata,* Giuseppe Verdi's romantic nineteenth-century opera about a tragic love affair that ends with a young courtesan's untimely death from tuberculosis.

Norman and Brown share an agent, and that agent suggested five-time Tony Award nominee Kelli O'Hara for the role of Francesca. O'Hara recruited Bartlett Sher, a Tony Award winner for his direction of *The Light in the Piazza, Awake and Sing!,* and a revival of *South Pacific* (in which O'Hara starred as Nellie Forbush), to direct the production (Raymond). Steven Pasquale, who starred as Robert Kincaid, had also worked with O'Hara before; they had co-starred in *Far from Heaven,* the 2013 musical adaptation of the 2002 film, at Playwrights Horizons off Broadway.

During the three and a half years Brown and Norman worked on the show, the process was highly collaborative: "Marsha wrote a first act, and when songs came up, she would either write a monologue or she would write a bunch of stage directions, or she would just leave a blank space and say, 'You do your thing here.' I would write a draft of a song, and in the course of the draft, I might change her dialogue, and I might change her stage directions, and I might change everything about everything and send it back to her. And she would generally say, 'Oh, this is great. Let me do this.' And she would fix the changes that I had made and make them better" (Evans 45). Norman has since described Brown as a genius, suggesting the respect was mutual.

Set in Winterset, Iowa, in 1965, *The Bridges of Madison County* is a story of a lushly romantic interlude in two otherwise melancholy lives. Francesca had come to Iowa as an Italian war bride with her G.I. husband, Bud Johnson, eighteen years earlier. She married Bud after her sweetheart, Paolo, was killed in the war. On Bud's Iowa farm, she has lived as a traditional midcentury housewife, cooking, cleaning, and raising two children, Michael and Carolyn. As the musical opens, Bud, Michael, and Carolyn all travel to Indianapolis to show Carolyn's steer in a national competition, leaving Francesca on her own for four days. When Robert Kincaid, a photographer on assignment for *National Geographic* magazine, comes to her house to ask for directions to a nearby covered bridge, she offers to ride over with him in his car to show him how to get there. As Norman has said, "This is a bridge that Francesca has to cross in order to get to the next part of her life" (Raymond). The two quickly fall into a passionate four-day love affair, one that severely tempts Francesca to leave her family to join him. But she finds herself unable to abandon them and finally decides to stay.

One reviewer has aptly described the critically disparaged book on which the musical is based as *Fifty Shades of Vanilla* (Brantley, "Hearts Ache"). That did not particularly bother Norman, who has said, "I like having a project where there's something for me to do. I got to fill in the town. I got to fill in the husband's story. I got to fill in the relationship with the children, so what you see is a big family story in the middle of which this incredible romance happens" (Evans 44).

"The book isn't really sophisticated, but the musical is," observed Elizabeth Stanley, the actress playing Francesca in the touring production (Moss E2). Norman has described the musical's theme as a series of questions: "What if you had a week that didn't count? What if you discovered your soulmate in the middle of a fading marriage and having children? What would you do?" (Evans 45). While the novel focused primarily on Robert, the musical focuses on Francesca, whose dilemma fits with Norman's favorite theme of the "trapped girl," as Norman has repeatedly acknowledged in interviews (Green, "Bridges"; Raymond).

Norman's version emphasizes how much Francesca misses her hometown of Naples, the most heavily bombed Italian city in World War II, and her sister. Francesca also talks wistfully about her sketching and her earlier wish to develop and use her artistic talent. Norman was very aware that the twentieth-century women's movement began with the publication of Betty Friedan's book

The Feminine Mystique in 1963, just two years before the time period of the musical (Reich). Francesca's frustrated yearnings and restlessness in small-town America were typical of those of a generation of women: "her entry into an adulterous situation seem[s] less about the betrayal of a husband she loves than about the accidental rediscovery of a lost part of herself" (Rooney).

Part of what traps Francesca is the perpetual surveillance she is under as her inquisitive neighbors scrutinize her every move. The neighbors sit on chairs around the edges of the stage action and move furniture and other properties on and off the stage. More than one reviewer noted that the show's staging evoked memories of Thornton Wilder's *Our Town* (see, for example, Brantley, "Heart Aches"; Geier; Rooney; and Soloski).

In the only scholarly approach to the musical, Valerie Accetta suggests that Norman's use of traditional musical theater conventions, such as the addition of the comedic neighbors, the chorus of community members, and the chronological storytelling (rather than the nonlinear storytelling of the source novel) distract from the romantic relationship at the heart of the musical, emphasizing the sordidness of the affair and making Francesca's sacrifice seem like a shameful and unduly public moment rather than the private renunciation it is in the novel.

Norman suggests, however, that the presence of the community in the play is more complicated than that: "The neighbors are there not only because we need them storytelling-wise; I'm very interested in how the observers of people in love are really under pressure about how to respond" (Raymond). Certainly Francesca's neighbor Marge shifts unexpectedly from critical to supportive and even protective. Sher, the director, has said, "The community is present, but it is never malevolent. I think what I find most quietly subversive is the way the community responds so atypically to Francesca" (Raymond).

The Bridges of Madison County premiered at the Williamstown Theatre Festival in Massachusetts in August 2013. The musical, shortened by about twelve minutes (Hetrick, "Brief"), then opened at the Gerald Schoenfeld Theatre on Broadway on February 20, 2014, and ran for 137 performances, including previews, and closed on May 18 of that year, before launching an eight-month national tour starting, appropriately enough, in Des Moines, Iowa, in November 2015.

Reviews were mixed. Jesse Green wrote a glowing review of the musical for *New York* magazine ("Everything's Up to Date"). Writing in the *New York Times,* Ben Brantley praised O'Hara's performance but was less enamored of the rest of the production. Similarly, Robert Zoglin, writing for *Time* magazine, praised the show's performances and score but suggested it lacked emotional impact. Other equivocal reviews included those by Elysa Gardner for *USA Today,* Mark Kennedy for the Associated Press, Peter Marks for the *Washington Post,* and Alexis Soloski for the *Guardian*.

Nevertheless, the musical was nominated for four Tony Awards and won two, for best original score and best orchestrations. It was also nominated for nine Drama Desk Awards, including outstanding book of a musical for Norman, and won two, outstanding orchestrations and outstanding music, for Brown.

WORKS CITED

Plays and Other Writings by Marsha Norman

"Anne Pitoniak." *Marsha Norman*. 30 April 2005. http://Marshanorman.com/2005/04/03/anne-pitoniak. Accessed Nov. 5, 2018.

"Articles of Faith: An Interview with Lillian Hellman." *American Theatre,* May 1984, 44–47. Rpt. in *The American Theatre Reader: Essays and Conversations from* American Theatre *Magazine.* Ed. by the staff of *American Theatre* magazine. New York: Theatre Communications Group, 2009. 364–70.

"Audrey Hepburn." 1999. TS. Alden Library, Ohio University, Athens, Ohio.

"Can Playwriting Be Taught?" *Dramatist* 9.1 (2006): 6–9. EBSCOhost. http://search.ebscohost.com/login.aspx?direct=true&db=ibh&AN=22322191&site=ehost-live.

Fortune Teller. New York: Random House, 1987.

Getting Out: A Play in Two Acts. New York: Dramatists' Play Service, 1979.

The Holdup. New York: Dramatist's Play Service, 1987.

Introduction. *Women Writing Plays: Three Decades of the Susan Smith Blackburn Prize.* Ed. Alexis Green. Austin: University of Texas Press, 2006. 1–7.

Last Dance. New York: Samuel French, 2004.

"Lillian Hellman's Gift to a Young Playwright." *New York Times,* August 26, 1984.

Lunch with Ginger. EST Marathon 1994: One-Act Plays. Ed. Marisa Smith. Lyme, N.H.: Smith and Kraus, 1995. 123–30.

"Marsha Norman and Donald Margulies: A Life in the Theatre." With Donald Margulies. *The Dramatist* 14.2 (2011): 22–35. EBSCOhost. http://search.ebscohost.com/login.aspx?direct=true&db=ibh&AN=76127093&site=ehost-live. Accessed November 7, 2018.

Marsha Norman: Collected Works. Vol. 1. Lyme, N.H.: Smith and Kraus, 1998.

'night, Mother. New York: Noonday, 1983.

"Not There Yet: What Will It Take to Achieve Equality for Women in the Theatre?" *American Theatre,* November 2009, 28–30, 79.

140. Love's Fire: Seven New Plays Inspired by Seven Shakespearean Sonnets. By Eric Bogosian, William Finn, John Guare, Tony Kushner, Marsha Norman, Ntozake Shange, and Wendy Wasserstein. New York: Morrow, 1998. 31–41.

Samantha: An American Girl Holiday. Middleton, Wisconsin: Pleasant Company Publications, 2004.

The Secret Garden. New York: Theatre Communications Group, 1982.

Third and Oak: The Laundromat. New York: Dramatist's Play Service, 1980.

Third and Oak: The Pool Hall. New York: Dramatist's Play Service, 1985.

Traveler in the Dark. New York: Dramatist's Play Service, 1984.

Trudy Blue. Humana Festival '95: The Complete Plays. Ed. Marisa Smith. Lyme, N.H.: Smith and Kraus, 1995. 223–76.

Trudy Blue. New York: Samuel French, 1996.

"Wendy Wasserstein: 1950–2006." *American Theatre,* April 2006, 20–21. *EBSCOhost,* sinclair.ohionet.org:80/login?url=https://search.ebscohost.com/login.aspx?direct=true&db=ibh&AN=20411080&site=ehost-live. Accessed September 5, 2015.

"Writing Plays Is an Act of Faith." *New York Times,* June 23, 1985. https://www.nytimes.com/1985/06/23/theater/writing-plays-is-an-act-of-faith.html. Accessed September 5, 2015.

Secondary Sources

Accetta, Valerie. "Framing *The Bridges of Madison County.*" *Studies in Musical Theatre* 8.2 (2014): 185–94.

Adler, Andrew. "Sets Set Tone in Norman's New Musical." *Louisville Courier-Journal,* April 26, 1991, 3, 10. Newspapers.com. https://www.newspapers.com/image/110124351/?terms=Norman%2C%2BMarsha. Accessed October 16, 2015.

———. "'This Very Organization Saved Me': Playwright Credits Arts Council with Starting Career." *Louisville Courier-Journal,* December 9, 1995. Newspapers.com. https://www.newspapers.com/newspage/111758919/. Accessed October 16, 2015.

Andrews, Suzanna. "Arthur Miller's Vanishing Act." *Vanity Fair,* September 13, 2007, 252–65. https://www.vanityfair.com/culture/2007/09/miller200709. Accessed May 10, 2016.

Athanassakis, Apostolos N. *The Homeric Hymn to Demeter.* Baltimore: Johns Hopkins University Press, 1976.

Authorized (King James) Version of the Bible. Cambridge University Press, n.d. Bible Gateway. https://www.biblegateway.com/. Accessed September 1, 2015.

Axton, W. F. Rev. of *The Fortune Teller. Louisville Courier-Journal,* May 24, 1987: 12. Newspapers.com. https://www.newspapers.com/image/109858351/?terms=Axton%2C%2BW.F.%2B%2BNorman%2C%2BMarsha. Accessed October 16, 2015.

Barbour, David. "Women of the House." *Hackensack (N.J.) Record,* April 21, 1991. NewsBank, 1991, PER 61:G10–13.

Barnes, Clive. "Contrary Mary and a Host of Ghosts." *New York Post,* April 26, 1991. NewsBank, 1991, PER 62:A2.

Beattie, L. Elisabeth, ed. "Marsha Norman." In *Conversations with Kentucky Writers.* Lexington: University Press of Kentucky, 1996. 282–97.

Bednerik, Marya. "Writing the Other." *Marsha Norman: A Casebook.* New York: Garland, 1996. 145–58.

Benedict, David. "Theatre Review: *Love's Fire,* the Pit, the Barbican." *London Independent,* May 26, 1998. https://www.independent.co.uk/life-style/theatre-review-loves-fire-the-pit-the-barbican-seven-scenes-of-bardic-love-1157346.html. Accessed October 22, 2015.

Betsko, Kathleen, and Rachel Koenig. *Interviews with Contemporary Women Playwrights.* New York: Beech Tree Books, 1987. 324–42.

Bigsby, Christopher. "Marsha Norman." *Contemporary American Playwrights.* New York: Cambridge University Press, 1999. 210–51.

Bixler, Phyllis. "Gardens, Houses, and Nurturant Power in *The Secret Garden.*" *Romanticism and Children's Literature in Nineteenth-Century England.* Ed. James Holt McGavran, Jr. Athens: University of Georgia Press, 1991. 208–24.

———. "The Secret Garden 'Misread': The Broadway Musical as Creative Interpretation." *Children's Literature* 22 (1994): 101–23.

Brantley, Ben. "Earthy Liaisons, Magnolia Scented." *New York Times,* June 4, 2003. https://www.nytimes.com/2003/06/04/theater/theater-review-earthy-liaisons-magnolia-scented.html. Accessed April 6, 2016.

———. "Hearts Ache in the Heartland: 'Bridges of Madison County' Brings Iowa to Broadway." *New York Times,* February 20, 2014. https://www.nytimes.com/2014/02/21/theater/bridges-of-madison-county-brings-iowa-to-broadway.html. Accessed March 21, 2016.

Breding, Connie J. "Communication and Family Roles: Mother-Daughter Talk in Marsha Norman's *'night, Mother.*" *North Dakota Journal of Speech and Theatre* 7.1 (1994): 73–83. Communication and Mass Media Complete. http://sinclair.ohionet.org:80/login?url=https://search.ebscohost.com/login.aspx?direct=true&db=ufh&AN=23872246&site=ehost-live. Accessed October 6, 2015.

Brode, Douglas. *The Films of Steven Spielberg.* New York: Citadel, 1995.

Brontë, Charlotte. *Jane Eyre.* 1847. Ed. Richard J. Dunn. New York: Norton, 1971.

Browder, Sally. "'I Thought You Were Mine': Marsha Norman's *'night, Mother.*" *Mother Puzzles: Daughters and Mothers in Contemporary American Literature.* Ed. Mickey Pearlman. New York: Greenwood, 1987. 109–13.

Brown, Janet, and Catherine Barnes Stevenson. "Fearlessly 'Looking Under the Bed': Marsha Norman's Feminist Aesthetic in *Getting Out* and *'night, Mother.*" *Theatre and Feminist Aesthetics.* Ed. Karen Laughlin and Catherine Schuler. Cranbury, N.J.: Associated University Presses, 1995. 182–99.

Brown, Linda Ginter. "A Place at the Table: Hunger as Metaphor in Lillian Hellman's *Days to Come* and Marsha Norman's *'night, Mother.*" *Modern Dramatists: A Casebook of Major British, Irish, and American Playwrights.* Ed. Kimball King. New York: Routledge, 2001. 177–94.

———. "More with Marsha Norman." *Marsha Norman: A Casebook.* Ed. Linda Ginter Brown. New York: Garland, 1996. 197–220.

———. "Update with Marsha Norman." *Marsha Norman: A Casebook.* Ed. Linda Ginter Brown. New York: Garland, 1996. 163–95.

———, ed. *Marsha Norman: A Casebook.* New York: Garland, 1996.

Brugnoli, Annalisa. "Marsha Norman." *The Methuen Drama Guide to Contemporary American Playwrights.* Ed. Martin Middeke, Peter Paul Schnierer, Christopher Innes, and Matthew C. Roudané. London: Bloomsbury, 2014. 224–42.

Brustein, Robert. "Marsha Norman in Conversation with Robert Brustein." *Broadway Song & Story: Playwrights/Lyricists/Composers Discuss Their Hits.* Ed. Otis L. Guernsey, Jr. New York: Dodd, Mead, 1985. 184–96.

Burke, Sally. "Precursor and Protégé: Lillian Hellman and Marsha Norman." *Southern Women Playwrights: New Essays in Literary History and Criticism.* Ed. Robert L. Macdonald and Linda Rohrer Paige. Tuscaloosa: University of Alabama Press, 2002. 103–23.

Burkman, Katherine H. "The Demeter Myth and Doubling in Marsha Norman's *'night, Mother.*" *Modern American Drama: The Female Canon.* Ed. June Schlueter. Rutherford, N.J.: Fairleigh Dickinson University Press, 1990. 254–63.

Burnett, Frances Hodgson Burnett. *The Secret Garden.* Ed. Gretchen Holbrook Gerzina. New York: Norton, 2006.

Campbell, Mary. "'The Pool Hall' Takes Its Cue on A&E Cable." *Los Angeles Times,*

October 29, 1989. http://articles.latimes.com/1989-10-29/news/tv-17_1_pool-hall. Accessed May 10, 2016.

Cash, Johnny. "I Walk the Line." *Johnny Cash and His Hot and Blue Guitar.* Memphis: Sun Record Co., 1957. MP3.

Ceneskie, Jill. "*Lunch with Ginger:* An Experiment with Environmental Theatre." Honors thesis, Otterbein College, 2001.

Chen, Wei-Huan. "Metaphors of *Secret Garden* Remain Secret." *Houston Chronicle.* Hearst Newspapers, 13 Oct. 2017. https://www.houstonchronicle.com/entertainment/arts-theater/article/Metaphors-of-Secret-Garden-remain-secret-12276766.php. Accessed Nov. 7, 2018.

Cline, Gretchen. "The Impossibility of Getting Out: The Psychopolitics of the Family in Marsha Norman's *Getting Out.*" *Marsha Norman: A Casebook.* Ed. Linda Ginter Brown. New York: Garland, 1996. 3–25.

The Color Purple: The Musical. 2015. https://colorpurple.com. Accessed December 27, 2017.

Cooperman, Robert. "'I Don't Know What's Going to Happen in the Morning': Visions of the Past, Present, and Future in *The Holdup.*" *Marsha Norman: A Casebook.* Ed. Linda Ginter Brown. New York: Garland, 1996. 95–107.

Craig, Carolyn Casey. "Marsha Norman: Getting Out the Truth about Family and Self." *Women Pulitzer Playwrights: Biographical Profiles and Analyses of the Plays.* Jefferson, N.C.: McFarland, 2004. 166–83.

Croce, James. "Bad, Bad Leroy Brown." *Life and Times.* New York: R2M Music, 1973. MP3.

Darr, Katheryn Pfisterer. *Far More Precious Than Jewels: Perspectives on Biblical Women.* Louisville, Ky.: Westminster/John Knox Press, 1991.

"David Lindsay-Abaire Named Co-Director of Juilliard's Playwrights Program." *American Theatre,* March 17, 2016. https://www.americantheatre.org/2016/03/17/david-lindsay-abaire-named-co-director-of-juilliards-playwrights-program/. Accessed December 27, 2017.

Demastes, William W. "American New Realism in the Theatre of the 80s." Ph.D. diss. University of Wisconsin–Madison, 1966.

———. *Beyond Naturalism: A New Realism in American Theatre.* New York: Greenwood, 1988.

———. "Jessie and Thelma Revisited: Marsha Norman's Conceptual Challenge in *'night, Mother.*" *Modern Drama* 36.1 (1993): 109–19.

DeVries, Hilary. "Marsha Norman's 'Traveler' Stumbles into a Pedantic Wilderness." *Christian Science Monitor,* February 22, 1984, 19. LexisNexis. https://advance-lexis-com.sinclair.ohionet.org/api/permalink/50e3f0bc-7184-4495-9532-d848a37e0278/?context=1516831. Accessed September 22, 2015.

DiGaetani, John L. "Marsha Norman." *A Search for a Postmodern Theater: Interviews with Contemporary Playwrights.* Greenwood, 1991. 245–51.

Dolan, Jill. Dolan, Jill. *The Feminist Spectator as Critic.* Ann Arbor: UMI Research Press, 1988.

———. Rev. of *'night, Mother. Women and Performance: A Journal of Feminist Theory* 1.1 (1983): 78–79.

"Donner Memorial State Park." California Department of Parks and Recreation, 2014. https://www.parks.ca.gov/pages/503/files/DonnerMemorialSPFinalWebLayout2017.pdf. Accessed Nov. 5, 2018.

Drew, Anne Marie. "'And the Time for It Was Gone': Jessie's Triumph in *'night, Mother.*" *Marsha Norman: A Casebook*. Ed. Linda Ginter Brown. New York: Garland, 1996. 87–94.

Edmundson, Paul, and Stanley Wells. *Shakespeare's Sonnets*. Oxford, U.K.: Oxford University Press, 2004.

Edney, Kathryn. "Adapting and Integrating: *The Color Purple* as Broadway Musical." *Alice Walker's* The Color Purple. Amsterdam: Rodopi, 2009. 225–47.

Epstein, Grace. "At the Intersection: Configuring Women's Difference in Norman's *Third and Oak: The Laundromat*." *Marsha Norman: A Casebook*. Ed. Linda Ginter Brown. New York: Garland, 1996. 27–46.

Evans, Suzy. "Bridge of Tears." *American Theatre,* February 2014, 44–47. EBSCOhost. http://search.ebscohost.com/login.aspx?direct=true&db=ibh&AN=93620451&site=ehost-live. Accessed November 9, 2018.

Evett, Marianne. "A Beautiful Musical with a Mystique." *Cleveland Plain Dealer,* April 28, 1991, 8H.

Fahy, Thomas Richard. *Freak Shows and the Modern American Imagination: Constructing the Damaged Body from Willa Cather to Truman Capote*. New York: Palgrave Macmillan, 2006.

Faragher, John Mack. *Daniel Boone: The Life and Legend of an American Pioneer.* New York: Holt, 1992.

Farley, Helen. *A Cultural History of Tarot: From Entertainment to Esotericism*. London: L. B. Tauris, 2009.

Finkle, David. "*Last Dance*." *TheaterMania*, June 3, 2003. https://www.theatermania.com/off-broadway/news/last-dance_3581.html. Accessed April 6, 2016.

Fitzgerald, F. Scott. *The Crack-Up*. Ed. Edmund Wilson. New York: New Directions, 1945.

FitzGerald, Michael Ray. "The Indianized White Man and the Anglicized Indian: Imperial and Anti-Imperial Discourse in NBC's *Daniel Boone,* 1964–1970." *Journal of American Culture* 37.3 (2014): 281–89.

Forman, Robert J., and Jenny S. Spencer. "Marsha Norman." *Critical Survey of Drama*. 2nd rev. ed. Ed. Carl Rollyson and Frank N. Magill. Hackensack, N.J.: Salem, 2003. 2488–94.

Frye, Northrop. *Anatomy of Criticism: Four Essays*. Princeton, N.J.: Princeton University Press, 1973.

Funderburg, Lise. *The Color Purple: A Memory Book of the Broadway Musical*. New York. Carroll & Graf, 2006.

Gallo, Phil. Rev. of *The Audrey Hepburn Story*. *Variety,* March 26, 2000. https://variety.com/2000/tv/reviews/the-audrey-hepburn-story-1200460884/. Accessed October 22, 2015.

Gardner, Elysa. "Well-cast 'Bridges' Burned by Cliché and Contrivance." *USA Today,* February 21, 2014. Academic Search Complete. http://sinclair.ohionet.org:80/login?url=https://search.ebscohost.com/login.aspx?direct=true&db=a9h&AN=JoE204307138714&site=ehost-live. Accessed October 6, 2015.

Garrison, Gary. "Interview with Marsha Norman." *Dramatist,* November/December 2007, 38–42. EBSCOhost. http://search.ebscohost.com/login.aspx?direct=true&db=ibh&AN=27774735&site=ehost-live. Accessed November 9, 2018.

Gates, Anita. "Television Review; First You Split, Then You Get It Together." *New York Times* August 20, 1999. https://www.nytimes.com/1999/08/20/movies/television-review-first-you-split-then-you-get-it-together.html. Accessed May 10, 2016.

Geier, Thom. Rev. of *The Bridges of Madison County. Entertainment Weekly* 21 Feb. 2014. ew.com/article/2014/02/21/bridges-madison-county-ew-review/. Accessed Nov. 5, 2018.

Gener, Randy. "Lynne Meadow's Next Stage: Tempering Passion with Practicality, She Steers Manhattan Theatre Club to a Berth on Broadway." *American Theatre,* December 2003, 18–22. Literary Reference Center. http://search.ebscohost.com.sinclair.ohionet.org/login.aspx?direct=true&db=lkh&AN=11567385&site=lrc-plus. Accessed April 6, 2016.

Gerard, Jeremy. "Review: 'The Red Shoes.'" *Variety,* December 26, 1993. variety.com/1993/film/reviews/the-red-shoes-2–1200434625/. Accessed May 10, 2016.

Gerzina, Gretchen Holbrook. "When Mary Met Cathy: Frances Hodgson Burnett in Brontë Country." *Frances Hodgson Burnett's* The Secret Garden: *A Children's Classic at 100.* Ed. Jackie C. Horne and Joe Sutliff Sanders. Lanham, Md.: Children's Literature Association and Scarecrow Press, 2011. 23–41.

Goldner, Nancy. "Two Views of 'The Red Shoes': The Dancing, At Least, Has Arresting Moments." *Philadelphia Inquirer,* December 19, 1993. http://www.articles.philly.com/1993-12-19/entertainment/25941569_1_national-ballet-lar-lubovitch-pennsylvania-ballet. Accessed May 10, 2016. http://www.philly.com/philly/archives/

Gooding, Miranda. "'Garden Doesn't Grow on this Kid." *New York Daily News,* May 29, 1991. NewsBank, 1991, PER 75: B14.

Gornik, April. "Marsha Norman." *BOMB,* Spring 2000. https://bombmagazine.org/articles/marsha-norman/. Accessed October 16, 2015.

Green, Jesse. "'The Bridges of Madison County' Heads to Broadway with a Fresh Female Perspective." *Elle,* December 28, 2013. https://www.elle.com/culture/music/interviews/a13929/marsha-norman-interview/. Accessed May 10, 2016.

———. "Everything's Up to Date in Madison County." *New York,* March 10, 2014, 134–36. Academic Search Complete. Accessed May 10, 2016.

Green, Judith. "'Shoes' Steps into History as an All-time Flop." *Chicago Tribune,* December 22, 1993. http://articles.chicagotribune.com/1993-12-22/news/9312220218_1_red-shoes-lar-lubovitch-ringing-and-funny-girl. Accessed May 10, 2016.

Greiff, Louis K. "Fathers, Daughters and Spiritual Sisters: Marsha Norman's *'night, Mother* and Tennessee Williams's *The Glass Menagerie.*" *Text and Performance Quarterly* 9.3 (1989): 224–28. *International Bibliography of Theatre and Dance with Full Text.* EBSCOhost. http://sinclair.ohionet.org:80/login?url=https://search.ebscohost.com/login.aspx?direct=true&db=ibh&AN=9320541&site=ehost-live

Groover, D.L. "*The Secret Garden* Offers Beautiful Voices Swathed in a Predictable Plot." *HoustonPress.* Houston Press, 13 Oct. 2017. https://www.houstonpress.com/arts/franks-pizza-owner-solves-a-small-town-mystery-11005437. Accessed Nov. 7, 2018.

Gussow, Mel. "A Surgeon's Crisis of Faith in a Marsha Norman Work." *New York Times,* January 16, 1990. https://www.nytimes.com/1990/01/16/theater/review-theater-a-surgeon-s-crisis-of-faith-in-a-marsha-norman-work.html. Accessed September 22, 2015.

———. "Critic's Notebook; Louisville Banquet of One-Act Plays." *New York Times,* November 24, 1983. https://www.nytimes.com/1983/11/24/arts/critic-s-notebook-louisville-banquet-of-one-act-plays.html?pagewanted=all. Accessed December 10, 2015.

———. "Entering the Mainstream: The Plays of Beth Henley, Marsha Norman, and Wendy Wasserstein." *Women Writing Plays: Three Decades of the Susan Smith Blackburn Prize.* Ed. Alexis Greene. Austin: University of Texas Press, 2006. 45–53.

———. "Women Playwrights: New Voices in the Theater." *New York Times Magazine,* May 1, 1983. https://www.nytimes.com/1983/05/01/magazine/women-playwrights-new-voices-in-the-theater.html?pagewanted=all. Accessed August 29, 2015.

Harbin, Billy J., and Jill Stapleton Bergeron. "Marsha Norman (1947–)." *Contemporary Poets, Dramatists, Essayists, and Novelists of the South: A Bio-Bibliographical Sourcebook.* Ed. Robert Bain and Joseph M. Flora. Westport, Conn.: Greenwood, 1994. 388–95.

"Harpo, Is That You? Oprah Winfrey, Steven Spielberg to Adapt 'The Color Purple' Musical into a Film." WJFA, 6. Nov. 2018. http://www.classichitsandoldies.com/v2/97150/ Accessed November 12, 2018.

Harriott, Esther. *American Voices: Five Contemporary Playwrights in Essays and Interviews.* Jefferson, N.C.: McFarland, 1988.

Hatcher, Jeffrey. *The Art & Craft of Playwriting.* Cincinnati: Story Press, 1996.

Hemingway, Ernest. *The Complete Short Stories of Ernest Hemingway: The Finca Vigía Edition.* New York: Scribner, 1987.

Hempel, Amy. "My Mother the Clairvoyant." *New York Times,* May 24, 1987. https://www.nytimes.com/1987/05/24/books/my-mother-the-clairvoyant.html. Accessed April 4, 2016.

Henry, William A., III. "Blasted Garden." *Time,* February 27, 1984, 9.

———. "A Children's Haven of Healing." *Time,* May 6, 1991, 75. Academic Search Complete. http://sinclair.ohionet.org:80/login?url=https://search.ebscohost.com/login.aspx?direct=true&db=a9h&AN=57879467&site=ehost-live. Accessed November 9, 2018.

Hetrick, Adam. "Brief Encounter with *The Bridges of Madison County* Writer Marsha Norman." *Playbill,* February 14, 2014. http://www.playbill.com/article/playbillcoms-brief-encounter-with-the-bridges-of-madison-county-writer-marsha-norman-com-214951. Accessed September 9, 2015.

Highland, Nathalie M. "Process, Style and Character in *The Secret Garden.*" Thesis, Bowling Green State University, 1994.

Hinson, Scott. "The 'Other Funeral': Narcissism and Symbolic Substitution in Marsha Norman's *Traveler in the Dark.*" *Marsha Norman: A Casebook.* Ed. Linda Ginter Brown. New York: Garland, 1996. 109–20.

Hulbert, Dan. "Though Beautiful, 'The Secret Garden' Lacks Youthful Allure." *Atlanta Journal,* May 6, 1991. NewsBank, 1991, PER 75:B12.

Innes, Kari-Anne. "Revelations of a Genealogy: Biblical Women in Performance during Twentieth-Century American Feminisms." Diss., Bowling Green State University, May 2012. https://scholarworks.bgsu.edu/theatre_diss/24/. Accessed March 11, 2016.

Isherwood, Charles. Rev. of *Last Dance. Variety,* June 3, 2003, 38. https://variety.com/2003/legit/reviews/last-dance-3-1200541312/. Accessed April 6, 2016.

———. Rev. of *Trudy Blue. Variety,* December 7, 1999. https://variety.com/1999/legit/reviews/trudy-blue-1117759838/. Accessed October 16, 2015.

Jafari, Alieyh Alsadat, and Shahram Kiaei. "Lacanian Psychoanalytical Theories in Marsha Norman's *'night, Mother.*" *International Journal of Applied Linguistics and English Literature* 4.3 (2015): 138–43. http://www.journals.aiac.org.au/index.php/IJALEL/article/viewFile/1292/1279. Accessed April 26, 2016.

James, Susan E. "*Wuthering Heights* for Children: Frances Hodgson Burnett's *The Secret Garden.*" *Connotations: A Journal for Critical Debate* 10.1 (2000–2001): 59–76.

http://www.connotations.de/article/susan-e-james-wuthering-heights-for-children-frances-hodgson-burnetts-the-secret-garden/. Accessed March 9, 2016.

Johnson, Malcolm. "Music, Casting Problems Take 'Red Shoes' Off Stage." *Hartford Courant,* December 26, 1993. http://articles.courant.com/1993-12-26/entertainment/0000000214_1_boris-lermontov-red-shoes-emeric-pressburger. Accessed March 10, 2016.

Jones, Chris. "In 'Bridges' on Broadway, Passions Remain Covered." *Chicago Tribune,* February 21, 2014. http://www.chicagotribune.com/entertainment/theater/chi-bridges-madison-county-review-column.html. Accessed March 21, 2016.

Kakutani, Michiko. "Books of the Times." *New York Times,* May 13, 1987. https://www.nytimes.com/1987/05/13/books/books-of-the-times-182787.html. Accessed January 25, 2016.

Kane, Leslie. "The Way Out, the Way In: Paths to Self in the Plays of Marsha Norman." *Feminine Focus: The New Women Playwrights.* Ed. Enoch Brater. New York: Oxford University Press, 1989. 255–74.

Kauffman, Stanley. "More Trick than Tragedy." *Saturday Review,* September–October 1983, 47–48. http://www.unz.com/print/SaturdayRev-1983oct-00047/?View=PDF. Accessed April 26, 2016.

Kelleher, Terry. "Picks & Pans: Tube." *People,* August 28, 2000, 34. Academic Search Complete. http://sinclair.ohionet.org:80/login?url=https://search.ebscohost.com/login.aspx?direct=true&db=a9h&AN=3454171&site=ehost-live. Accessed May 10, 2016.

———. Rev. of *Samantha: An American Girl Holiday. People,* November 29, 2004, 42. *Academic Search Complete.* EBSCOhost. http://search.ebscohost.com/login.aspx?direct=true&db=a9h&AN=15148036&site=ehost-live. Accessed May 10, 2016.

Kennedy, Mark. "Score Soars in 'Bridges of Madison County.'" *New York Times,* February 20, 2014. https://www.nytimes.com/aponline/2014/02/20/arts/ap-us-theater-review-the-bridges-of-madison-county.html. Accessed September 5, 2015.

Kentucky Colonels: Kentucky's Ambassadors of Good Will and Fellowship. https://www.kycolonels.org/. Accessed May 13, 2016.

Keyser, Elizabeth Lennox. "'Quite Contrary': Frances Hodgson Burnett's *The Secret Garden.*" *Children's Literature* 11 (1983): 191–207.

King, Alice. Rev. of *A Cooler Climate. Entertainment Weekly,* December 15, 2000. http://www.ew.com/topic/cooler-climate. Accessed May 10, 2016.

Kintz, Linda. *The Subject's Tragedy: Political Poetics, Feminist Theory, and Drama.* Ann Arbor: University of Michigan Press, 1992.

Kirkus Media. Rev. of *The Fortune Teller. Kirkus Reviews,* May 1, 1987. https://www.kirkusreviews.com/book-reviews/marsha-norman/the-fortune-teller-2/. Accessed September 28, 2015.

Klein, Alvin. "theater; 'Sarah and Abraham,' 2 Plays at Once." *New York Times,* February 16, 1992. *New York Times,* 2015. https://www.nytimes.com/1992/02/16/nyregion/theater-sarah-and-abraham-2-plays-at-once.html. Accessed September 28, 2015.

Kramer, Mimi. "The Key to the Garden." *New Yorker,* May 13, 1991, 84–85.

Kroll, Jack. "Broadway Hothouse." *Newsweek,* May 6, 1991, 89.

———. "A Modern Crisis of Faith." *Newsweek,* February 27, 1984, 76.

Kundert-Gibbs, John. "Revolving It All: Mother-Daughter Pairs in Marsha Norman's *'night, Mother* and Samuel Beckett's *Footfalls.*" *Marsha Norman: A Casebook.* Ed. Linda Ginter Brown. New York: Garland, 1996. 47–62.

Lawson, Carol. "Broadway." *New York Times,* November 11, 1983. https://www.nytimes.com/1983/11/11/arts/broadway.html. Accessed December 10, 2015.

The Lilly Awards. N.d. http://thelillyawards.org/. Accessed December 10, 2015.

Linan, Steven. "Even with Roles Reversed, Formula Wins in the End." *Los Angeles Times,* August 28, 2000. http://articles.latimes.com/2000/aug/28/entertainment/ca-11416. Accessed May 10, 2016.

Mackey, Margaret. "Strip Mines in the Garden: Old Stories, New Formats, and the Challenge of Change." *Children's Literature in Education* 27.1 (1996): 3–22. Literary Reference Center. Accessed May 5, 2016.

Mall, Janice. "*Fortune Teller* by Marsha Norman." *Los Angeles Times,* June 21, 1987. http://articles.latimes.com/1987-06-21/books/bk-8717_1_marsha-norman. Accessed October 16, 2015.

Marks, Peter. "Broadway's 'Bridges of Madison County' Opens." *Washington Post,* February 20, 2014. https://www.washingtonpost.com/news/arts-and-entertainment/wp/2014/02/20/broadways-bridges-of-madison-county-opens/?utm_term=.7ffd7dbd8f8c. Accessed March 21, 2015.

Marquis, Claudia. "The Power of Speech: Life in *The Secret Garden.*" *Journal of the Australasian Universities Language and Literature Association* 68 (November 1987): 163–87.

"Marsha Norman to Read from her Works Today at Kentucky Center for the Arts." *Louisville Courier-Journal,* March 5, 1989, 12. Newspapers.com. http://sinclair.ohionet.org:80/login?url=https://search.ebscohost.com/login.aspx?direct=true&db=a9h&AN=34541718&site=ehost-live. Accessed October 16, 2015.

McKerrow, Steve. "New Audiences Find New Meaning Emerges from 'Secret Garden.'" *Baltimore Sun,* February 15, 1994. http://articles.baltimoresun.com/1994-02-15/features/1994046147_1_landesman-secret-garden-archibald-craven. Accessed October 22, 2015.

McNulty, Charles. "To Be or Not to Be: Playwrights on the Complex Issue of Suicide." *Los Angeles Times,* August 18, 2014. http://www.latimes.com/entertainment/arts/la-et-cm-drama-and-suicide-mcnulty-20140818-column.html. Accessed September 5, 2015.

Mootz, William. "*D. Boone.*" *Louisville Courier-Journal,* February 28, 1992. Newspapers.com. https://www.newspapers.com/image/110119429. Accessed October 16, 2016.

———. "Marsha Norman Bounces Back: Undeterred by 'Red Shoes' Fiasco, Playwright Takes On Another Musical." *Louisville Courier-Journal,* April 24, 1994, 1, 6. Newspapers.com. https://courier-journal.newspapers.com/image/110085235. Accessed May 17, 2015.

———. "Marsha Norman is Back on Broadway." *Louisville Courier-Journal,* April 21, 1991: I-1, 7. Newspapers.com. https://courier-journal.newspapers.com/image/110120627. Accessed October 16, 2015.

———. "Marsha Norman to Unveil Excerpt from New Musical Called 'Winter Shakers.'" *Louisville Courier-Journal,* September 18, 1983, 11. Newspapers.com. https://courier-journal.newspapers. com/image/110620582. Accessed October 16, 2015.

———. Rev. of *Trudy Blue. Louisville Courier-Journal,* March 20, 1995. Newspapers.com. https://www.newspapers.com/newspage/110626368/. Accessed May 13, 2016.

Morris, Nigel. *The Cinema of Steven Spielberg: Empire of Light.* New York: Wallflower, 2007.

Myers, Victoria. "Marsha Norman." *The Interval: The Smart Girl's Guide to Theatricality.* November 21, 2014. https://the-interval.com/interviews/2014/11/19/marsha-norman/#.Vmmn6TZdHmQ. Accessed December 10, 2015.

Moss, Meredith. "'Bridges of Madison County' Is Coming to Schuster Center." *Dayton Daily News* 13 March 2016: E1-E2.

"Norman's *Trudy Blue* Extends at MCC Until Jan. 9." *Playbill,* December 8, 1999. http://www.playbill.com/news/article/normans-trudy-blue-extends-at-mcc-until-jan.-9–85850/print. Accessed October 16, 2015.

Orser, Joseph Andrew. *The Lives of Chang and Eng: Siam's Twins in Nineteenth-Century America.* Chapel Hill: University of North Carolina Press, 2014.

Pardi, Robert. Rev. of *The Audrey Hepburn Story. TV Guide,* 2000. www.tvguide.com/movies/the-audrey-hepburn-story/reviews/134748. Accessed Nov. 5, 2018.

Paul, Lissa. "Enigma Variations: What Feminist Theory Knows About Children's Literature." *Signal,* September 1987, 186–201.

Piazza, Roberta. "Dramatic Discourse Approached from a Conversational Analysis Perspective: Catherine Hayes's *Skirmishes* and Other Contemporary Plays." *Journal of Pragmatics* 31.8 (1999): 1001–23. OhioLINK Electronic Journal Center, https://rave.ohiolink.edu/ejournals/article/336915562.

Pringle, Peter. "Broadway Battle for the Soul of *The Red Shoes.*" *Independent,* December 11, 1993. https://www.independent.co.uk/news/world/broadway-battle-for-the-soul-of-the-red-shoes-1466860.html. Accessed May 19, 2016.

Radavich, David. "Marsha Norman's Bi-Regional Vision in *'night, Mother.*" *Mississippi Quarterly* 64.1/2 (2011): 115–28.

Raymond, Gerard. "An Affair to Remember." Broadway Direct, March 4, 2014. https://broadwaydirect.com/an-affair-to-remember/. Accessed September 9, 2015.

Reich, Ronni. " 'The Bridges of Madison County' Writer Marsha Normans Finds 'a good strong backbone for a musical.'" New Jersey Star-Ledger 2 Feb. 2014. www.nj.com/entertainment/arts/index.ssf/2014/02/the_bridges_of_madison_county_musical.html. Accessed Sept. 9, 2015.

"Religion in Prisons: A 50-State Survey of Prison Chaplains." Pew Research Center, March 22, 2012. http://www.pewforum.org/2012/03/22/prison-chaplains-exec/. Accessed September 1, 2015.

Reuning, Sarah. "Depression—the Undiagnosed Disability in Marsha Norman's *'night, Mother.*" *Peering Behind the Curtain: Disability, Illness, and the Extraordinary Body in Contemporary Theater.* Ed. Thomas Fahy and Kimball King. New York: Routledge, 2002. 55–67.

Rich, Adrienne. *Of Woman Born: Motherhood as Experience and Institution.* 10th anniversary ed. New York: Norton, 1986.

Rich, Frank. "'Garden': The Secret of Death and Rebirth." *New York Times,* April 26, 1991. https://www.nytimes.com/1991/04/26/theater/review-theater-garden-the-secret-of-death-and-birth.html?pagewanted=all. Accessed September 5, 2015.

———. "Suicide Talk in *'night, Mother.*'" *New York Times* April 1, 1983. https://www.nytimes.com/1983/04/01/theater/theater-suicide-talk-in-night-mother.html? Accessed September 5, 2015.

Richards, David. "Sunday View; Only the Wind Should Sigh in This 'Garden.'" *New York Times,* May 5, 1991, 5, 29. https://www.nytimes.com/1991/05/05/theater/sunday-view-only-the-wind-should-sigh-in-this-garden.html?. Accessed March 18, 2016.

———. "Review/Theater: The Red Shoes; Ambition vs. Romance in a Pas de Trois." *New York Times,* December 17, 1993. https://www.nytimes.com/1993/12/17/theater/review-theater-the-red-shoes-ambition-vs-romance-in-a-pas-de-trois.html. Accessed March 10, 2016.

Ridley, Clifford A. "'The Secret Garden' in New York." *Philadelphia Inquirer,* April 26, 1991. NewsBank, 1991, PER 62:A3.

Rooney, David. "*The Bridges of Madison County:* Theater Review." *Hollywood Reporter,* February 20, 2014. https://www.hollywoodreporter.com/review/bridges-madison-county-theater-review-682092. Accessed March 21, 2016.

"Roscolux." Rosco Laboratories website, 2016. https://us.rosco.com/en. Accessed February 16, 2016.

Rose, Lacey. "Oprah Winfrey on Closing Harpo Studies, OWN Expansion, Broadway Plans (Exclusive)." *Hollywood Reporter,* March 3, 2015. https://www.hollywoodreporter.com/news/oprah-winfrey-closing-harpo-studios-778784. Accessed September 5, 2015.

Rosefeldt, Paul. *The Absent Father in Modern Drama.* New York: Peter Lang, 1995. Print.

Rosenberg, Howard. "Feel-Good Ending Betrays Field, Davis in 'Climate.'" *Los Angeles Times,* August 21, 1999. http://articles.latimes.com/1999/aug/21/entertainment/ca-2190. Accessed May 10, 2016.

Rubik, Margarete. "A Sisterhood of Women: Marsha Norman's *Getting Out* and *The Laundromat.*" *Gramma: Journal of Theory and Criticism* 2 (1994): 141–47.

Sanoff, Alvin P. "Tarot Cards Catch the Eye of a Master Writer." *U.S. News and World Report,* June 8, 1987, 78.

Savran, David. "Marsha Norman." *In Their Own Words: Contemporary American Playwrights.* New York: Theatre Communications Group, 2988. 178–92.

Scharine, Richard G. "Caste Iron Bars: Marsha Norman's *Getting Out* as Political Theatre." *Women in Theatre.* Ed. James Redmond. Cambridge University Press, 1989. 185–98.

Shapiro, Laura, and Marc Peyser. "A Corpse de Ballet Classic." *Newsweek,* December 27, 1993. Academic Search Complete. Accessed May 10, 2016.

Silver, Anna Krugovoy. "Domesticating Brontë's Moors: Motherhood in *The Secret Garden.*" *The Lion and the Unicorn* 21.2 (1997): 193–203. Project Muse. https://muse-jhu-edu.proxy.ohiolink.edu:9100/article/35349. Accessed Nov. 9, 2018.

Simmons, Ira. "Marsha Norman Hopes to Stay on Top of Wheel of Fortune with Her First Novel." *Louisville Courier-Journal,* May 3, 1987, I1, I9. Newspapers.com. https://www.newspapers.com/image/110107128/. Accessed October 16, 2015.

Simon, John. "Marsha Norman's *Trudy Blue.*" *New York,* December 20, 1999, 164. http://nymag.com/nymetro/arts/theater/reviews/1685/#print. Accessed October 16, 2015.

———. "Southern Comforts." *New York,* June 16, 2003, 102. http://nymag.com/nymetro/arts/theater/reviews/n_8780/#print. Accessed April 6, 2016.

Smith, Raynette Halvorsen. "'*night, Mother* and *True West:* Mirror Images of Violence and Gender." *Violence in Drama.* Ed. James Redmond. New York: Cambridge University Press, 1991. 277–89.

Soloski, Alexis. "*The Bridges of Madison County: The Broadway Musical*—Review." *Guardian,* February 20, 2014. https://www.theguardian.com/stage/2014/feb/21/bridges-of-madison-county-broadway-musical-review. Accessed March 21, 2016.

Southgate, Patsy. "Marsha Norman: Writing about the Big Questions." *East Hampton Star,* May 21, 1998. http://easthamptonstar.com/Archive/2/Marsha-Norman-Writing-About-Big-Questions. Accessed September 5, 2015.

Spencer, Jenny S. "Marsha Norman's She-Tragedies." *Making a Spectacle: Feminist*

Essays on Contemporary Women's Theatre. Ann Arbor: University of Michigan Press, 1989. 147–65.

———. "Norman's *'night, Mother:* Psycho-Drama of Female Identity." *Modern Drama* 30.3 (1987): 364–75.

Stanley, Alessandra. "The Doll That Became a Movie (No, Not Chucky)." *New York Times,* November 23, 2014. nytimes.com/2004/11/23/arts/television/the-doll-that-became-a-movie-no-not-chucky.html. Accessed May 10, 2016.

———. "Marsha Norman Finds Her Lost Key to Broadway." *New York Times,* April 21, 1991, H5, H33. https://www.nytimes.com/1991/04/21/theater/theater-marsha-norman-finds-her-lost-key-to-broadway.html?pagewanted=all. Accessed March 18, 2016.

———. "Patients in Therapy, Therapist in Trouble." *New York Times* 2 April 2009. nytimes.com/20009/04/03/arts/television/03trea.html. Accessed Nov. 5, 2018.

Steadman, Susan M. "Norman, Marsha." *Notable Women in the American Theatre.* Ed. Alice M. Robinson, Vera Mowry Roberts, and Milly S. Barranger. Westport, Conn.: Greenwood, 1989. 691–95.

Stoddart, Helen. *Rings of Desire: Circus History and Representation.* Manchester, U.K.: Manchester University Press, 2000.

Stone, Elizabeth. "Playwright Marsha Norman: An Optimist Writes about Suicide, Confinement and Despair." *Ms.,* July 1983, 56–59.

Stout, Kate. "Marsha Norman Writing for the 'Least of Our Brethren.'" *Saturday Review,* September/October 1983, 28–33. http://www.unz.com/print/SaturdayRev-1983oct-00028. Accessed September 5, 2015.

Tennyson, Lord Alfred. *In Memoriam.* Ed. Robert H. Ross. New York: Norton, 1973.

Theatre for Humans. United Nations, 2015. https://www.theatreforhumans.com/. Accessed December 10, 2015.

Thompson, David S. "'I'm . . . Marsha Norman': Behind the Scenes with the Pulitzer Prize-Winning Playwright." *Southern Theatre* 48.3 (2007): 10–14.

Thwaite, Ann. *Waiting for the Party: The Life of Frances Hodgson Burnett.* Boston: Godine, 1991.

Tompkins, Jane. *West of Everything: The Inner Life of Westerns.* New York: Oxford University Press, 1992.

Trible, Phyllis. *Texts of Terror: Literary-Feminist Readings of Biblical Narratives.* Philadelphia: Fortress, 1984.

Tucker, Ken. Rev. of *The Audrey Hepburn Story. Entertainment Weekly* 31 March 2000. Ew.com/article/2000/03/31/Audrey-hepburn-story-2/. Accessed November 5, 2018.

Ullom, Jeffrey. *The Humana Festival: The History of New Plays at the Actors Theatre of Louisville.* Carbondale: Southern Illinois University Press, 2008.

Walker, Alice. *The Same River Twice: Honoring the Difficult.* New York: Scribner, 1996.

Wattenberg, Richard. "Feminizing the Frontier Myth: Marsha Norman's *The Holdup.*" *Modern Drama* 33.4 (1990): 507–17.

Watts, Patti. "Staged for Success." *Executive Female,* March/April 1991, 24–25, 40.

Weales, Gerald. "Lost in Translation: 'The Secret Garden(s).'" *Commonweal,* June 14, 1991, 405–06.

———. "Coming Apart: *Marriage* and *Sarah and Abraham.*" *Commonweal,* April 10, 1992, 18–19. Academic Search Complete. http://sinclair.ohionet.org:80/login?url=https://search.ebscohost.com/login.aspx?direct=true&db=a9h&AN=9204272308&site=ehost-live. Accessed October 6, 2015.

Weber, Bruce. "What Went So Wrong with 'The Red Shoes.'" *New York Times,* December 30, 1993. https://www.nytimes.com/1993/12/30/theater/what-went-so-very-wrong-with-red-shoes.html?pagewanted=all. Accessed May 10, 2016.

Weeks, Jerome. "A 'Secret' Revealed." *Dallas Morning News,* June 15, 1992. NewsBank, 1992, PER 86:C9.

Wiles, Timothy. "Suicide and Self-Annihilation: Marsha Norman's *'night, Mother* and Karen Finley's *The Constant State of Desire.*" *Staging the Rage: The Web of Misogyny in Modern Drama.* Ed. Katherine H. Burkman and Judith Roof. Madison, N.J.: Fairleigh Dickinson University Press, 1988. 112–23.

Wilhelm, Albert E. "Marsha Norman. *The Fortune Teller* (Book)." *Library Journal,* April 15, 1987, 100. Literary Reference Center Plus. Accessed April 4, 2016.

Wilmeth, Don B., and Christopher Bigsby. *The Cambridge History of American Theatre.* Cambridge, U.K.: Cambridge University Press, 2000.

Winship, Frederick M. "'Red Shoes' Are a Poor Fit as a Broadway Musical." UPI, December 17, 1993. https://upi.com/Archives/1993/12/17/Red-Shoes-are-a-poor-fit-as-a-Broadway-musical/654576104400. Accessed May 9, 2016.

Zoglin, Richard. "*The Bridges of Madison County* Soars on Broadway." *Time,* February 21, 2014. http://entertainment.time.com/2014/02/21/bridges-of-madison-county-musical-broadway/. Accessed March 21, 2016.

INDEX